Library of
Davidson College

Leadership For Dynamic State Economies

A Statement by the
Research and
Policy Committee of
the Committee for
Economic Development

ALABAMA
ALASKA
ARIZONA
ARKANSAS
CALIFORNIA
COLORADO
CONNECTICUT
DELAWARE
FLORIDA
GEORGIA
HAWAII
IDAHO
ILLINOIS
INDIANA
IOWA
KANSAS
KENTUCKY
LOUISIANA
MAINE
MARYLAND
MASSACHUSETTS
MICHIGAN
MINNESOTA
MISSISSIPPI
MISSOURI
MONTANA
NEBRASKA
NEVADA
NEW HAMPSHIRE
NEW JERSEY
NEW MEXICO
NEW YORK
NORTH CAROLINA
NORTH DAKOTA
OHIO
OKLAHOMA
OREGON
PENNSYLVANIA
RHODE ISLAND
SOUTH CAROLINA
SOUTH DAKOTA
TENNESSEE
TEXAS
UTAH
VERMONT
VIRGINIA
WASHINGTON
WEST VIRGINIA
WISCONSIN
WYOMING

338.973
C734l

Library of Congress Cataloging-in-Publication Data

86-10290

Committee for Economic Development. Research and
    Policy Committee.
    Leadership for dynamic state economies.

    1. United States — Economic policy. 2. Industry and
state — United States — States. 3. Intergovernmental fiscal
relations — United States. I. Title.
HC103.C734   1986   338.973   86-20760
ISBN   0-87186-782-6
ISBN   0-87186-082-1 (pbk.)

First printing in bound-book form: 1986
Paperback: $9.50
Library binding: $11.50
Printed in the United States of America
Design: Stead Young & Rowe Inc.

COMMITTEE FOR ECONOMIC DEVELOPMENT
477 Madison Avenue, New York, N.Y. 10022
(212) 688-2063
1700 K Street, N.W., Washington, D.C. 20006
(202) 296-5860

CONTENTS

RESPONSIBILITY FOR CED STATEMENTS ON NATIONAL POLICY	vi

PURPOSE OF THIS STATEMENT	ix

CHAPTER 1 INTRODUCTION AND SUMMARY	1
Economic Federalism	2
The New State Activism	4
State Economic Strategy	5
State Economic Institutions	8
The Emerging State Role	9

PART I: STRATEGY	10
CHAPTER 2 DIAGNOSIS: ASSESSING THE POTENTIAL	12
Dynamics of the State Economy	12
Broader Economic Trends	14
Potential for State Action	18
Monitoring and Evaluation	24

CHAPTER 3 VISION: SETTING DIRECTION	28
Fostering a Vital Private Sector	29
Facilitating Change	30
Building Economic Foundations	31
Dealing Pragmatically with Competitive Challenges	35
Enhancing Regional Economies	37

CHAPTER 4 ACTION: GETTING THERE	39
Human Resources	39
Physical Infrastructure	43
Natural Resources	44
Knowledge and Technology	46
Enterprise Development	47
Quality of Life	51
Fiscal Management	52

PART II: INSTITUTIONS — 54

CHAPTER 5 LEADERSHIP: TAKING PERSONAL INITIATIVE — 56
An Economic Leadership Checklist — 56
The Governor and Executive Branch — 58
The Legislature — 60
Business — 62
Local Government — 65
Media — 66
Other Important Institutions — 67

CHAPTER 6 PARTNERSHIP: LINKING COMMON INTERESTS — 68
Partnership within State Government — 68
Public-Private Partnership — 69
Government-Industry-University Partnership — 73
Federal-State Partnership — 77
State-Local Partnership — 80
State-to-State Partnership — 84
Civic Partnership — 85

MEMORANDA OF COMMENT, RESERVATION, OR DISSENT — 88

APPENDIXES — 92
Appendix A: Distribution of Tennessee, Massachusetts, and U.S. Earnings by Industries, 1983 — 92
Appendix B: State Government Actions that Affect Economic Foundations — 94
Appendix C: The Evolution of Economic Development Agencies — 101

LIST OF RESEARCH STUDIES PREPARED FOR THIS REPORT — 103

OBJECTIVES OF THE COMMITTEE FOR ECONOMIC DEVELOPMENT — 104

Leadership
For
Dynamic
State
Economies

RESPONSIBILITY FOR CED STATEMENTS ON NATIONAL POLICY

The Committee for Economic Development is an independent research and educational organization of over two hundred business executives and educators. CED is nonprofit, nonpartisan, and nonpolitical. Its purpose is to propose policies that will help to bring about steady economic growth at high employment and reasonably stable prices, increase productivity and living standards, provide greater and more equal opportunity for every citizen, and improve the quality of life for all. A more complete description of CED appears on page 104.

All CED policy recommendations must have the approval of trustees on the Research and Policy Committee. This Committee is directed under the bylaws to "initiate studies into the principles of business policy and of public policy which will foster the full contribution by industry and commerce to the attainment and maintenance" of the objectives stated above. The bylaws emphasize that "all research is to be thoroughly objective in character, and the approach in each instance is to be from the standpoint of the general welfare and not from that of any special political or economic group." The Committee is aided by a Research Advisory Board of leading social scientists and by a small permanent professional staff.

The Research and Policy Committee does not attempt to pass judgment on any pending specific legislative proposals; its purpose is to urge careful consideration of the objectives set forth in this statement and of the best means of accomplishing those objectives.

Each statement is preceded by extensive discussions, meetings, and exchange of memoranda. The research is undertaken by a subcommittee, assisted by advisors chosen for their competence in the field under study. The members and advisors of the subcommittee that prepared this statement are listed on page viii.

The full Research and Policy Committee participates in the drafting of recommendations. Likewise, the trustees on the drafting subcommittee vote to approve or disapprove a policy statement, and they share with the Research and Policy Committee the privilege of submitting individual comments for publication, as noted on pages 88 through 90 of this statement.

Except for the members of the Research and Policy Committee and the responsible subcommittee, the recommendations presented herein are not necessarily endorsed by other trustees or by the advisors, contributors, staff members, or others associated with CED.

RESEARCH AND POLICY COMMITTEE

Chairman
WILLIAM F. MAY

Vice Chairmen
ROY L. ASH/*National Economy*
WILLIAM S. EDGERLY/*Education and Social and Urban Development*
RODERICK M. HILLS/*Improvement of Management in Government*
JAMES W. McKEE, JR./*International Economic Studies*

*ROY L. ASH
Los Angeles, California

*RALPH E. BAILEY, Chairman and Chief Executive Officer
Conoco Inc.

ROBERT H. B. BALDWIN, Chairman, Advisory Board
Morgan Stanley & Co. Incorporated

WARREN L. BATTS, President
Dart & Kraft, Inc.

JACK F. BENNETT, Senior Vice President
Exxon Corporation

THEODORE A. BURTIS, Chairman of the Board
Sun Company, Inc.

OWEN B. BUTLER, Retired Chairman
The Procter & Gamble Company

FLETCHER L. BYROM, Retired Chairman
Koppers Company, Inc.

ROBERT J. CARLSON, Chairman, President and Chief Executive Officer
BMC Industries Inc.

RAFAEL CARRION, JR., Chairman of the Board
Banco Popular de Puerto Rico

JOHN B. CAVE
Summit, New Jersey

ROBERT A. CHARPIE, President
Cabot Corporation

ROBERT CIZIK, Chairman and President
Cooper Industries, Inc.

EMILIO G. COLLADO, Executive Chairman
International Planning Corporation

RONALD R. DAVENPORT, Chairman of the Board
Sheridan Broadcasting Corporation

PETER A DEROW, President
CBS/Publishing Group

FRANK P. DOYLE, Senior Vice President
General Electric Company

W. D. EBERLE, President
Manchester Associates, Ltd.

WILLIAM S. EDGERLY, Chairman
State Street Bank and Trust Company

THOMAS J. EYERMAN, Partner
Skidmore, Owings & Merrill

JOHN H. FILER, Partner
Tyler, Cooper & Alcorn

EDMUND B. FITZGERALD, Chairman and Chief Executive Officer
Northern Telecom Limited

ROBERT F. FROEHLKE, Chairman of the Board
Equitable Life Assurance Society of the United States

DONALD E. GUINN, Chairman and Chief Executive Officer
Pacific Telesis Group

RICHARD W. HANSELMAN, Former Chairman
Genesco Inc.

PHILIP M. HAWLEY, Chairman of the Board
Carter Hawley Hale Stores, Inc.

ROBERT C. HOLLAND, President
Committee for Economic Development

LEON C. HOLT, JR., Vice Chairman and Chief Administrative Officer
Air Products and Chemicals, Inc.

JAMES L. KETELSEN, Chairman and Chief Executive Officer
Tenneco Inc.

CHARLES M. KITTRELL, Executive Vice President
Phillips Petroleum Company

PHILIP M. KLUTZNICK, Senior Partner
Klutznick Investments

RALPH LAZARUS, Chairman Emeritus
Federated Department Stores, Inc.

*FRANKLIN A. LINDSAY, Chairman
Vectron, Inc.

WILLIAM F. MAY, President
Statue of Liberty – Ellis Island Foundation, Inc.

ALONZO L. McDONALD, Chairman and Chief Executive Officer
Avenir Group, Inc.

JAMES W. McKEE, JR., Chairman
CPC International Inc.

ROBERT E. MERCER, Chairman of the Board
The Goodyear Tire & Rubber Company

RUBEN F. METTLER, Chairman of the Board and Chief Executive Officer
TRW Inc.

STEVEN MULLER, President
The Johns Hopkins University

NORMA PACE, Senior Vice President
American Paper Institute

CHARLES W. PARRY, Chairman and Chief Executive Officer
Aluminum Company of America

DEAN P. PHYPERS, Senior Vice President
IBM Corporation

HAROLD A. POLING, President
Ford Motor Company

LELAND S. PRUSSIA, Chairman of the Board
BankAmerica Corporation

*JAMES Q. RIORDAN, Vice Chairman and Chief Financial Officer
Mobil Corporation

FRANCIS C. ROONEY, JR., Chairman of the Board
Melville Corporation

*HENRY B. SCHACHT, Chairman of the Board and Chief Executive Officer
Cummins Engine Company, Inc.

DONNA E. SHALALA, President
Hunter College

ROCCO C. SICILIANO, Of Counsel
Jones, Day, Reavis & Pogue

PHILIP L. SMITH, President and Chief Operating Officer
General Foods Corporation

ROGER B. SMITH, Chairman
General Motors Corporation

*ELMER B. STAATS, Former Comptroller General of the United States
Washington, D.C.

WILLIAM C. STOLK
Bridgeport, Connecticut

MORRIS TANENBAUM, Executive Vice President
AT&T

ANTHONY P. TERRACCIANO, Vice Chairman, Global Banking
The Chase Manhattan Bank, N.A.

WALTER N. THAYER, Chairman
Whitney Communications Company

W. BRUCE THOMAS
Vice Chairman of Administration and Chief Financial Officer
USX Corporation

SIDNEY J. WEINBERG, JR., Partner
Goldman, Sachs & Co.

RICHARD D. WOOD, Chairman, President and Chief Executive Officer
Eli Lilly and Company

WILLIAM S. WOODSIDE, Chairman
American Can Company

---

*Voted to approve the policy statement but submitted memoranda of comment, reservation, or dissent. (See page 88.)

SUBCOMMITTEE ON STATE ECONOMIC PROGRESS

Chairman
WILLIAM S. EDGERLY
Chairman
State Street Bank and Trust Company

ALAN S. BOYD
Chairman
Airbus Industrie of North America

WILLIAM H. BRICKER
Chairman, President and
 Chief Executive Officer
Diamond Shamrock Corporation

HUGH M. CHAPMAN
President
The Citizens and Southern
 Corporation

DOUGLAS D. DANFORTH
Chairman
Westinghouse Electric Corporation

GEORGE C. DILLON
Chairman of the Board
Butler Manufacturing Company

EDWIN D. DODD
Chairman Emeritus
Owens-Illinois, Inc.

JOHN T. DORRANCE, JR.
Chairman of the Executive
 Committee
Campbell Soup Company

THOMAS J. EYERMAN
Partner
Skidmore, Owings & Merrill

DAVID C. FARRELL
Chairman and Chief Executive Officer
The May Department Stores Company

DONALD E. GARRETSON
Community Service Executive Program
3M Company

JOHN D. GRAY
Chairman Emeritus
Hartmarx Corp.

JAMES M. KEMPER, JR.
Chairman of the Board
Commerce Bancshares, Inc.

PHILIP M. KLUTZNICK
Senior Partner
Klutznick Investments

CHARLES F. KNIGHT
Chairman and Chief Executive Officer
Emerson Electric Co.

FRANCIS P. LUCIER
Mohawk Data Sciences Corporation

GEORGE F. MOODY
President and Chief Executive Officer
Security Pacific National Bank

BARBARA W. NEWELL
Lecturer on Education
Harvard University

CHARLES W. PARRY
Chairman and Chief Executive Officer
Aluminum Company of America

BURNELL R. ROBERTS
Chairman and Chief Executive Officer
The Mead Corporation

RALPH S. SAUL
Financial Consultant
Philadelphia, Pennsylvania

ROCCO C. SICILIANO
Of Counsel
Jones, Day, Reavis & Pogue

SHERWOOD H. SMITH, Jr.
Chairman and President
Carolina Power & Light Company

G. J. TANKERSLEY
Chairman
Consolidated Natural Gas
 Company

WAYNE E. THOMPSON
Past Chairman
Merritt Peralta Medical Center

J. KELLEY WILLIAMS
President
First Mississippi Corporation

THOMAS R. WILLIAMS
Chairman
First Wachovia Corporation

RICHARD D. WOOD
Chairman, President and
 Chief Executive Officer
Eli Lilly and Company

Nontrustee Member*

ROBERT R. KILEY
Chairman, Metropolitan
 Transportation Authority
State of New York

*Nontrustee members take part in all discussions of the statement but do not vote on it.

ADVISORS

ALAN K. CAMPBELL
Vice Chairman
ARA Services, Inc.

BELDEN H. DANIELS
President
Counsel for Community
 Development

BERNARD L. GLADIEUX
Alexandria, Virginia

*DONALD HAIDER
Professor and Program Director
J. L. Kellogg Graduate School
 of Management
Northwestern University

DONALD F. MAZZIOTTI
Executive Director
Pennsylvania Business Roundtable

EDWIN S. MILLS
Professor of Economics
Princeton University

JOHN B. OLSEN
Senior Vice President
Mellon Bank, N.A.

FRANK W. SCHIFF
Consultant
CED, Washington

JAMES M. SOUBY
Director
The Council of State
 Planning Agencies

*member, Research Advisory Board

PROJECT DIRECTOR
R. SCOTT FOSLER
Vice President and Director
 of Government Studies
CED, Washington

PROJECT STAFF
JOHN J. FORRER
Senior Research Associate
CED, Washington

CAROL L. ALVEY
Administrative Assistant
CED, Washington

PROJECT EDITOR
SANDRA KESSLER HAMBURG
Associate Director of Information

PURPOSE OF THIS STATEMENT

Through the rest of this century, the United States will undoubtedly continue to face new and unprecedented challenges to its international competitiveness. While policy makers have chiefly focused on developing solutions to this problem at the national and corporate levels, CED's trustees feel that there has been inadequate appreciation of the fact that actions taken — or not taken — by our nation's fifty states can have important implications for the vitality of the U.S. economy as a whole.

Accordingly, the CED Subcommittee on State Economic Progress launched its study of this issue almost three years ago with two convictions. First, its members recognized that our federal form of government currently grants extensive and crucial decision-making authority to the states in almost every public policy arena affecting economic development. Second, the business leaders and experts on state development who took part in this study were acutely aware of how profoundly state-level actions can affect the productive and efficient operation of communities and the business and workers that operate in them.

Each state must now face up to some critical economic choices. In this policy statement, *Leadership for Dynamic State Economies,* we lay out what we believe are the most effective approaches state leaders can take to promote economic progress in their states. We hope that this policy statement will give impetus to public- and private-sector leaders in each state to move in these directions. We believe such actions can redound to the long-run benefit of their organizations, their states, and their country.

IMPROVING THE QUALITY OF GOVERNMENT

Since 1942, the Committee for Economic Development has worked to identify and promote policies that can increase the nation's economic competitiveness and provide enhanced opportunities for all of its citizens. CED's concern with the quality of state and local government dates back to the mid-1960s, when it issued several reports which reassessed the quality of state and local government and the delicate balance of the nation's federal system. In its 1976 report *Improving Productivity in State and Local*

Government, CED recognized that "state and local governments are a fundamental and integral part of our nation's overall economic well-being."

Ten years later, *Leadership for Dynamic State Economies* explores the process by which states can make the most effective use of their public and private resources to stimulate productive economic activity.

To be sure, the economic decisions made and implemented by states do not take place in a vacuum. Many factors limit a state's ability to make full use of its productive resources, not the least of which are national fiscal and monetary policy and global competition. But other factors over which states exercise important decision-making power can also impair the outcome of economic development strategies.

Leadership for Dynamic State Economies provides a framework for understanding how the interdependence of economic forces affects states and how they can relate the impact of these forces to their specific needs. As we see it, each state has the responsibility to evaluate and act upon issues that will — to a large extent — determine whether its economic climate is supportive of productive private business activity, job creation, and human resource development.

A DELICATE WEB OF INTERRELATIONSHIPS

Leadership for Dynamic State Economies highlights the important interrelationships that exist among the nation's three levels of government and their most pressing economic and social issues.

Many recent CED studies and those on its current agenda quite explicitly involve action at the level of state government. For example, the 1985 CED report *Investing in Our Children: Business and the Public Schools* pointed out that states have the ultimate responsibility for setting educational policy and ensuring that its schools provide the best possible education for all students. The quality of its human resources will have a powerful impact on each state's economic vitality.

However, in that report, CED also cautions states not to usurp arbitrarily the decision-making power of local communities, which have historically guided our public education system. Excessive regulation at the state level can often inhibit the development and implementation of innovative approaches to education reform. *Investing in Our Children* urges a "bottom-up" strategy for reforming public education so that reforms are designed and implemented where learning actually takes place — in the school, in the classroom, and in the interaction between teacher and student.

Similarly, *Public-Private Partnership: An Opportunity for Urban Communities* (1982) highlighted the critical role that business-government collaboration can play in economic development strategies at the local level. In the course of doing this study, CED increasingly realized how important state-level actions were becoming for developing meaningful solutions to local economic and social problems.

Several current CED studies also exemplify the dynamic role of states. Decisions made at the state level as well as at the federal level in the areas of health-care policy, labor market adjustment, risk management and dispute resolution, and agriculture policy will by and large determine whether public policies in these areas contribute to U.S. productivity and competitiveness.

A FOUNDATION OF RESEARCH

The recommendations contained in this report build on a strong foundation of research on specific state economic development practices. The Subcommittee commissioned in-depth case studies of four states which represent a diversity of American regions and varied but instructive approaches to economic development. In addition, several other case studies focus on specific state economic issues.

The in-depth case studies cover California, Massachusetts, Michigan, and Tennessee. Among the issues these case studies address are the history of economic development and job growth, trends in public-private cooperation, the relationship between economic growth and federal government actions, and the relationship between state and local governments.

Three other case studies were chosen because of a special approach each state took to a specific development issue. Indiana built new institutions for developing economic strategy; Minnesota emphasized the quality of public services as a key to economic development; and Arizona consciously tried to shift from an economy that relied on natural resources to one that stressed high technology. The case studies will be published next year as a companion volume to the policy statement. A list of these studies and their authors appears on page 103.

ACKNOWLEDGMENTS

On behalf of the Research and Policy Committee, I would like to express deep appreciation and thanks to William S. Edgerly, chairman of the State Street Bank and Trust Company of Boston. As chairman of the CED Subcommittee on State Economic Progress, he brought forthright and highly knowledgable leadership to a very complex set of issues.

Our thanks also go to the members of the Subcommittee who were so willing to share their time, experience, and knowledge. Their names appear on page viii.

Project Director R. Scott Fosler, CED's vice president and director of government studies, deserves special thanks for the insight, keen appreciation of the workings of state government, and technical expertise he brought to this project. We also would like to thank John J. Forrer, senior research associate at the Committee for Economic Development, and Carol Alvey, CED administrative assistant, for their important contribution to the report.

Many people in the public and private sectors throughout the country gave generously of their knowledge and advice in the preparation of this report, and to them we express our thanks.

We would also like to express our deep appreciation for the financial support given this project by The Ford Foundation and the Lilly Endowment, Inc.

William F. May
Chairman
Research and Policy Committee

Chapter 1

Introduction And Summary

ALABAMA
ALASKA
ARIZONA
ARKANSAS
CALIFORNIA
COLORADO
CONNECTICUT
DELAWARE

Powerful forces have thrust the fifty American states toward center stage in efforts to achieve the full potential of the U.S. economy. States whose leaders seize this opportunity will both strengthen their own economies and help the nation's economy to thrive in an era of global competition. States whose leaders fail to take the initiative or who succumb to quick fixes at the expense of long-term performance will be outpaced by those with greater vision and skill.

The primary energy and innovation for strong state and regional economies must come from the private sector. The key to economic vitality is a dynamic, innovative, and market-driven private sector. Business enterprises can improve their competitiveness in part by helping to strengthen the state and regional economies in which they operate. Private-sector leaders should act as full partners with the governments and citizens with whom they share a common destiny and help provide the leadership needed to achieve common goals. The private sector in each state needs good organization and good communications to perform in the state policy arena and for this purpose can draw on effective organizational approaches already proven at the local level.

State government officials need to assure that government policies facilitate change and support innovation in the private sector. Narrow or compartmentalized approaches to economic development are ill-suited to the new competitive environment. State government officials need to reach outside of government circles for help in shaping the vision and developing the know-how required. The climate is right to break the logjams that have impeded effective action in the past and to open a new era of economic opportunity at the state level.

ECONOMIC FEDERALISM

The new economic role for the states should be seen in the context of changing economic responsibilities at all three levels of government. The federal government's responsibility for fiscal, monetary, and foreign trade policies will be even more important as the United States becomes more deeply integrated with the world economy. Federal policies not only affect the national economy as a whole, but they can also have an uneven effect on individual regions and states.

Local governments are critical to national economic health for many of the same reasons that state governments are — they provide basic services, such as education, infrastructure, and natural resource management, that are critical to the functioning of the private sector.

The states possess significant powers that make them an increasingly important link in economic federalism[1] (see "State Powers that Affect Economic Development," page 3). They have a direct role in their own right. They also act as implementors of federal policy, utilizing federal financial support and contending with the constraints of federal regulations. And they affect the ability of local governments to do their jobs properly and look to local government to perform the many functions for local areas that the state government cannot hope to provide as efficiently.

States play a key role as pioneers. Because the best prescription for economic improvement is not always clear, there is a need for experimentation for which the states are an appropriate vehicle. For example, the 27 states that have established enterprise zones may collectively produce better results and more knowledge about how such zones best work than if the federal government had launched a nationwide enterprise zone program. Experimentation does not necessarily mean initiating new programs; it may mean modifying current policies, linking them with other efforts in the public or private sectors, or eliminating some programs altogether. We are skeptical, for example, of the utility of state government venture capital programs.

By tailoring approaches to their own circumstances, individual states are more likely to find solutions that work. When they succeed, other states can adopt their approaches. When they do not, the experience can be instructive, while the damage to the national economy is more limited.

---

1. We use the term "state" generally to refer to the geographical entity and political jurisdiction. For example, the "state of Alabama" refers to the land area, population, and institutions within the borders of Alabama, and to the legal political entity recognized in the U.S. Constitution. We use the term "state government" to mean specifically the formal government institutions established by the people of the state under the powers derived from the Constitution. Occasionally the term "state" is used as stylistic shorthand for "state government," although we attempt to maintain the distinction where it is important.

STATE POWERS THAT AFFECT ECONOMIC DEVELOPMENT

State public services are fundamental to the private sector. Such services include education, transportation, water supply, sewage treatment, health, employment exchange, and numerous others.

States have regulatory and adjudicatory powers. They regulate banking, insurance, telecommunications, professions and trades, land use, the environment, employment, health, occupational safety, labor, and consumer affairs.

State tax and spending decisions affect economic activity. State taxation and spending are substantial. In 1985, state and local personal income, sales, and property tax receipts were $375.0 billion (greater than federal personal income taxes of $351.1 billion); state and local purchases of goods and services were $460.7 billion, or 83 percent of all nondefense purchases by all levels of government (including the federal government).[a]

States can respond to conditions that vary by region. They can more readily take into account the special features of substate economic regions, especially those of metropolitan areas, that transcend the political boundaries of local government. States working together can deal more effectively with some aspects of interstate regional economic needs than the federal government can by imposing structures or solutions from above.

States can form partnerships among key economic players. The cooperation among government, business, labor, universities, and community groups that is required for economic growth in many cases can best be undertaken at the state level.

States can put together specific deals. They can bring together the tax, regulatory, financial, and technical assistance elements to assist firms, pursue joint ventures, or become their own land developers for economic projects.

Local government is a creature of the state. Local governments, which are critical to local economic vitality, depend upon states for the legal, structural, and financial ability to deal successfully with their economies.

States can experiment on a regional basis. As "laboratories of democracy," the many states acting individually are more likely to discover productive approaches than the federal government acting alone. Their individual failures are less likely to be as disruptive to the national economy.

a. *Economic Report of the President* (Washington, D.C.: U.S. Government Printing Office, 1986), p. 253.

THE NEW STATE ACTIVISM

The recent wave of state economic initiatives was stimulated by several forces, including the economic shocks of the 1970s, the recessions of the early 1980s, the de facto New Federalism of the Reagan administration, a new spirit of entrepreneurship and local business development, and the challenge of foreign competition. Other important trends reinforce the growing economic importance of states (see "Trends Affecting the State Economic Role," below).

In response to these forces, state governments have undertaken literally hundreds of efforts in such areas as venture capital, small-business incubation, education reform, infrastructure improvement, job training and placement, technological research and development, and export promo-

---

TRENDS AFFECTING THE STATE ECONOMIC ROLE

● Increased production capacity overseas has challenged the dominance of American industries and the economic strength of the regions where those industries are concentrated.

● Competitive advantage among places increasingly depends upon the better use of human resources, for which states have major responsibilities, rather than upon natural endowments.

● Sustained success requires an economic environment and institutions that promote the development and transformation of new technology into the production of marketable products.

● Economic restructuring has created disparities in the economic fortunes of regions within the same state.

● Suburban growth continues to transform the physical and economic structure of urban America, straining the administrative capacity of local institutions and creating pressure for a state response.

● Rising affluence has increased emphasis on the quality of life, both as an attraction to employees and as the basis of enterprises in recreation, entertainment and tourism.

● Expanding direct trade and investment links between American states and foreign economies are casting state governments as world political actors in their own right.

● Growing awareness by citizens that state governments have important responsibilities for economic performance will present a special challenge to state leaders confronted with economic stress.

tion.[2] Some of the initiatives are original, while others are replications of federal programs or the programs of other states. Some efforts will be successful. Others are likely to fail because they are poorly conceived, ineffectively executed, or stymied by other state actions. Some programs may actually retard economic development.

We have included numerous examples throughout this statement from every state in the union. Our intent in doing so is not to endorse the state actions which are cited individually or generically. Strategies, programs, and institutions cannot be properly evaluated outside of the economic and political context in which they operate. We include the examples to illustrate the wide range of actions under way and to demonstrate the need to evaluate the benefits and costs of those actions. The advantage in the next generation of state economic programs will probably go to those states that best sort the wheat from the chaff in the experience already at hand.

The wide range of actions reflects the challenge states face when so many things they do affect economic performance.* In most states, economic policy is simply the cumulative economic impact of such actions as changing the tax law, siting hazardous waste plants, funding new vocational education programs, or limiting liability claims. What state leaders need is a way to address the economic importance of such issues individually and to consider their collective impact on the long-term performance of the economy.

In this statement we suggest such an approach, the essence of which is summarized in the chart, "Guiding Principles for Improving State Economies," on page 6. It directs attention to both the substance of economic strategy and the institutions through which strategy is developed and implemented. The two — strategy and institutions — go hand in hand.

STATE ECONOMIC STRATEGY

States need an economic strategy that consists of a diagnosis of opportunities and risks, a vision for the future, and actions that are in accord with that vision. A wise state strategy does not entail setting out detailed, comprehensive economic plans that risk becoming bureaucratic or quickly outdated. Its purpose is to help leaders understand the dynamics of economic change, avoid or revise policies that could have undesirable

---

2. For a discussion of many of these initiatives see the following publications: National Governors' Association, *Technology & Growth: State Incentives in Technological Innovation* (Washington, D.C.: 1983); Congressional Office of Technology Assessment, United States Congress, *Technology, Innovation, and Regional Economic Development* (Washington, D.C.: 1984); President's Commission on Industrial Competitiveness, *Innovations in Industrial Competitiveness at the State Level*, prepared by SRI International (Menlo Park, California: December 1984); National Governors' Association, Center for Policy Research, *Revitalizing State Economies*, A Report to the Committee on Economic Development and Technological Innovation (Washington, D.C.: February 1986).

---

*See memorandum by ROY L. ASH (page 88).

GUIDING PRINCIPLES FOR IMPROVING STATE ECONOMIES

1) While the role of state government in the economy is limited, state actions can be decisive in shaping the way a state economy adjusts to the competitive world economy.

2) State government officials should recognize the fundamental importance of a dynamic, market-driven private sector and their role in supporting it, and private-sector leaders should recognize the important economic role of state government and assist in developing it.

3) States need a broadly conceived economic strategy to identify priority actions, to give cohesion to government actions, and to avoid actions which may be harmful to the economy.

4) A state economic strategy should consist of three major components:
   - **Diagnosis** of the state's economic potential that supplements traditional indicators with a deeper understanding of regional and international economic dynamics and which evaluates current policies in light of changing economic conditions.
   - **Vision** that aims to invigorate the market economy and create a climate conducive to entrepreneurship and development, to invest in building the economic foundations required for long-term performance, to facilitate change, and to deal pragmatically with outside competition. The vision should place economic objectives within the context of other goals that aim to provide economic opportunity and a better life for all.
   - **Actions** that are specific enough that they can be completed within a reasonable period of time and that someone can be held accountable for results.

5) New institutional structures and processes are required to deal with economic change, new political realities, and evolving knowledge. Two key ingredients of institutional change are the following:
   - **Leadership** from key individuals in government, business, labor, universities, and the media to energize and direct individual institutions toward productive economic action.
   - **Partnership** among institutions in both the public and private sectors and at various levels of government to link common interests and mobilize complementary capabilities to benefit the state economy as a whole.

economic consequences, and identify priority actions that are practical and mutually reinforcing. It should articulate direction and long-term goals but allow latitude for politically realistic short-term action.

Diagnosis should supplement conventional economic indicators such as per capita income, unemployment, and job creation with a broader consideration of world economic trends and a deeper understanding of regional economic dynamics. The sudden hardships confronted by states that until recently had benefited from strong economies based on oil and agriculture should caution against overlooking signs of change. The high technology resurgence of New England, which had been widely thought to be in a state of chronic decline due to the loss of its textile and shoe industries, serves as a reminder that the seeds of new growth may be obscured by conventional indicators. Major economic forces, including the growth of service and knowledge-based employment, technology-driven markets, and unprecedented world competition, are reshaping America's regional economies. State actions that fail to recognize these realities are likely to be futile or even counterproductive.

Vision is required to avoid tempting but self-defeating short-term actions and to harness the forces that can provide long-term advantage. We stress the importance of fostering a vital, market-driven private sector as the key to job creation and competitiveness. This is best achieved not through the conventional emphasis on recruiting firms *to* the state, but in creating an environment that facilitates change and is conducive to development and entrepreneurship *within* the state. The emphasis should be placed on freeing the energy, talent, and motivation in the private sector to compete and perform. In many instances, the most important thing state government can do is remove barriers to economic performance. However, state governments also have a role to play in building the foundations required for economic growth. They also need to deal pragmatically with the competition they face from outside the state.

Action compatible with the vision must be politically realistic. We believe priority should be given to investing in the foundations upon which the emerging economy depends. These foundations include:

- a capable and adaptable work force
- adequate physical infrastructure
- well-managed natural resources
- up-to-date knowledge and technology
- access to capital
- an attractive quality of life
- a sound fiscal base

State governments should recognize their key responsibilities in these areas and assure that their actions are mutually supportive and not working at cross purposes.

STATE ECONOMIC INSTITUTIONS

States need effective institutional arrangements for developing and implementing economic strategy. No economic theory or set of prescriptions, even if valid, can be directly applied to the diverse conditions of the fifty states. An economic strategy is based as much on political interests as on economic theory. It involves trade-offs among competing goals that require political resolution. In the end, a strategy will guide action only if numerous people and institutions understand it, share its vision, and work to accomplish it. In short, state economic strategy will be only as effective as the institutions and people who develop and implement it.

Common institutional deficiencies include the following:

- State economic policy is narrowly defined and tends to be equated with the state agency that bears the "economic development" label.
- Efforts at broader definition usually fail to be translated into a cohesive strategy or implemented in a coordinated fashion.
- Economic concerns are defined with an insufficient view to the long term.
- In the absence of a broader and longer-term perspective, de facto economic policy at the state level is determined by numerous isolated decisions and driven by individual administrative and political agendas.

To correct these deficiencies and provide the institutional framework needed for effective economic strategy will require leadership and partnership.

Leadership is required to assure that key institutions contribute to overall performance. The governor has a special responsibility, but other state leaders share that responsibility. This includes other government leaders, especially legislators, and leaders in the private sector, including business executives, university administrators and academicians, labor leaders, heads of nonprofit organizations, community and political leaders, and editors and journalists. Local government is one of the state's most important instruments of economic policy and should also be considered a key institution and source of leadership.

Partnerships are also required to link common economic interests among groups that have complementary goals, but that may otherwise be in conflict. Political skill is required to define a vision that encompasses the long-term interests of these groups and to forge the coalitions and strategic alliances needed for sustained and constructive effort.

Key partnerships include those:

- within the executive and legislative branches of state government and between those branches
- among institutions in the private sector
- between the public and private sectors
- among state government, universities, and industry
- among levels of government — federal and state, state and local, and state-to-state

THE EMERGING STATE ROLE

State economic responsibility, in sum, is a demanding matter. Strategy to carry out that responsibility is more than a package of financial incentives and promotional activities or a collection of all the latest programs. An effective state economic strategy requires **diagnosis** of opportunities and risks, a **vision** of the future, and pragmatic and politically realistic **action**. It requires institutions whose **leaders** are knowledgeable and effective and among which **partnerships** are forged to pursue common purposes.

The task of meeting our nation's economic challenge cannot be restricted to any one segment of society. The private sector bears the principal responsibility for entrepreneurial drive and productivity, and federal and local governments have major roles. But each state, mobilizing its own internal strengths, can help give the United States the edge it needs to achieve its full economic potential in an era of global competition.

Part I: Strategy

States need an economic strategy to help do the following:

- keep abreast of changing economic conditions
- account for conditions unique to the state
- set priorities among the numerous state government actions that are important to economic performance
- identify and curb actions harmful to economic performance
- coordinate related actions that have economic impact

A strategy implies neither the development of detailed plans nor a presumption to direct the activities of the private sector. To the contrary, a strategy is important precisely for the purpose of assuring that harmful, even if inadvertent, government action does not impede the development of a market-driven and competitive economy. Political dynamics and institutional inertia in many states are likely to work against long-run economic performance unless concerted action is taken to remove barriers and provide supports to foster a vital private sector.

In our view, the most sensible kind of state economic strategy is like using a *compass* to point direction rather than wandering aimlessly over uncharted territory or, at the other extreme, following a detailed road map that is well out of date. Thought needs to be given to the direction of the journey, but allowance must be made for the fact that the terrain is frequently rough and roadless, and that whatever markings exist on the surface may be misleading. The compass approach focuses government action on creating an environment in which a market-driven economy can flourish. It articulates long-term goals and direction but allows latitude for politically realistic short-term action.

State economic strategy should consist of three components which address key questions regarding the state economy:

- **Diagnosis** which asks: Where are we, where are events taking us, and where do we have the potential to go?

- **Vision** which asks: Where do we want to go, and what are our options for getting there?

- **Action** which asks: What steps should we take to get where we want to go?

The three components are not neatly distinguished from one another in practice. They overlap and are in play simultaneously. The important thing is that the questions associated with each be addressed and that the close relationship among them be recognized. The next three chapters analyze each of these three components.

Chapter 2

Diagnosis: Assessing The Potential

FLORIDA
GEORGIA
HAWAII
IDAHO
ILLINOIS
INDIANA
IOWA
KANSAS
KENTUCKY

Effective strategy begins with an understanding of the limits and the potential of the state economy.

DYNAMICS OF THE STATE ECONOMY

Conventional economic measures such as per capita income and employment by themselves do not capture the dynamism of the state economy (see "Better Indicators of the State Economy," page 13). During the 1960s and early 1970s for example, the New England economy was widely characterized as being in decline because of the loss of textile and other manufacturing industries. Hidden within the aggregate indicators, however, were the nascent activities of high technology and business and financial services. Since the mid-1970s, they have provided the engine of growth for a revitalized New England economy.

From 1979 to 1983, Michigan experienced its worst downturn since the depression of the 1930s, due to the decline in durable goods manufacturing. Yet, during that four-year period, some 2,304 new manufacturing firms were established in the state, whereas 2,161 were lost because they folded or relocated. Among those firms that stayed in business, 40 percent increased their employment, and average employment was up by over 50 percent.[1]

National data reveal similar dynamics. The 2 million net additional jobs that the national economy has averaged in recent years are the result of the creation of 6 million new jobs and the loss of 4 million old jobs. Of the losses, about half have been due to contractions and half to business fail-

---

1. John E. Jackson, "Economic Development in Michigan, Past or Future?" case study prepared for the Committee for Economic Development, August 1985, pp. 23-24.

ures. About half of the new jobs have been the result of expansion of existing firms, and about half have been created by new firms.[2]

Broad definitions of state or regional economies can also mask significant differences within those regions. The Tennessee economy, for example, is made up of at least three economic systems in the eastern, middle, and western parts of the state. Each part is more closely related to economic activities in adjacent states than it is to those in the other parts of Tennessee.

A state's economy is not a static entity to be defined by snapshot statistics. It is, rather, an evolutionary process, dynamic and changing, to be understood in all its dimensions. The complex origin of the automobile industry in Michigan is a case in point (see "Genesis of the Auto Industry in Michigan," page 15).

---

2. Catherine Armington and Margie Odle, "Formation and Growth of High-Technology Firms: A Regional Assessment," (Washington, D.C.: Harris and Associates, 1983).

BETTER INDICATORS OF THE STATE ECONOMY

There is no single indicator, or even a small set of indicators, that provides an unambiguous measure of the performance of state economies. Instead, each state must develop a set that best fits its particular economic structure and program needs. For example, some of the indicators that could be used to measure aspects of the state economy are:

- Overall Economic Performance: rate of long-term (more than 12 weeks) unemployment; growth in per capita income; traditional indicators such as housing starts, vehicle registrations, and tax revenues.

- Entrepreneurial Climate: rate of new business formation and failures; venture capital placements in state; research activity at universities; over-the-counter stock issues; growth rate of the number of self-employed.

- Long-Term Growth Prospects: rate of diversification of the economy during the past 10 years; measures of the performance of primary and secondary schools; reduction in illiteracy rate during the past 5 years; average educational attainment of the workforce.

- Other Aspects of a State's Wealth: infant mortality rate; change in air quality in major cities; change in water quality; poverty rate (after allowing for government transfers and in-kind benefits); crime rate.

SOURCE: Roger J. Vaughan, Robert Pollard, and Barbara Dyer, *The Wealth of States: Policies for a Dynamic Economy* (Washington, D.C.: Council of State Planning Agencies, 1986), p. 33.

BROADER ECONOMIC TRENDS

Several long-term trends justify and require effective economic strategies on the part of states.

CONTINUING MOVEMENT TOWARD SERVICE-, TECHNOLOGY-, AND KNOWLEDGE-BASED EMPLOYMENT

In 1776, most of the work force in the United States was engaged in agriculture. By 1907, a little over a century later, more workers were engaged in manufacturing than in farming. By 1957, a bare fifty years later, more workers were engaged in information processing than industrial activities.[3] In 1983, less than 2 percent of employee earnings in the United States were in agriculture, and less than 24 percent were in manufacturing (see Appendix A).

This shift in sectoral activity reflected dramatic improvements in productivity that generated enormous national wealth. The output of the agricultural and manufacturing sectors has not declined during the nation's 200-year history. Rather, it has continued to grow even as the sectors' relative shares of total employment have decreased. Higher productivity in agriculture and manufacturing left more people and capital available to perform services. Within the service sector, the professional, technical, and administrative jobs that rely heavily on knowledge have been growing more rapidly than traditional service jobs in transportation, utilities, and trade.

The transformation to a service-based employment has occurred in every region of the country, even those historically dependent on agriculture and manufacturing. In 1983, for example, workers in Tennessee agriculture accounted for little over 1 percent of total earnings in the state, less than the national average. For all of the differences between the economies of Massachusetts and Tennessee, in neither state did workers derive more than 30 percent of total earnings from manufacturing (see Appendix A). Michigan's manufacturing output by 1985 had recovered to levels it had attained before the 1980 and 1981-1982 recessions, but more than 100,000 manufacturing workers were still without jobs.

Disparities in the distribution of wealth among the states have also diminished.

- In 1929, eighteen states had per capita incomes below 75 percent of the national average. By 1981, only one state, Mississippi, was below 75 percent.

---

3. Edgar S. Dunn, Jr., *The Development of the U.S. Urban System, Volume II: Industrial Shifts, Implications* (Washington, D.C.: Resources for the Future, Inc., 1983), p. 177.

- In 1929, ten states had incomes 25 percent greater than the national average. By 1981, only Alaska and the District of Columbia had per capita incomes that were 25 percent higher.

- In 1929, per capita income in the poorest state, South Carolina, was 23 percent of that of the richest state, New York. By 1981, the lowest state's per capita income was 62 percent of that of the highest.[4]

---

4. Bernard L. Weinstein, Harold T. Gross, and John Rees, *Regional Growth and Decline in the United States* (New York: Praeger, 1985), pp. 49-52.

GENESIS OF THE AUTO INDUSTRY IN MICHIGAN

By all rights, the American automobile industry should have developed in New England, where there was a strong manufacturing base, machine tool industry, substantial capital, and investors and entrepreneurs eager to market the automobile. In fact, the Duryea Motor Wagon Company was manufacturing a gasoline engine automobile in Springfield, Massachusetts, in 1896, several years before any Michigan firm.

Several important elements, however, converged in Michigan to spur the growth of the auto industry. Numerous mechanics in southeastern Michigan were familiar with the internal-combustion gasoline engine, which was widely used in marine transportation on the Great Lakes. Five of the principal auto entrepreneurs—Ransom Olds, Henry Ford, Henry Leland, and the Dodge brothers—all had firsthand experience with the engine. Marine transportation had developed to ship the state's valuable natural resources, principally timber and iron. Also critical to the development of the automobile were the carriage makers, wheelwrights, and machine shops that served the railroad industry in Michigan. The railroads, in turn, had been attracted by the state's natural resources and the potential for tourism. Michigan also had ample capital, particularly in the form of personal fortunes made in the lumber and furniture industries, and Michigan's investors were seeking new growth opportunities.

Even with all these elements present, it was not inevitable that the automobile industry would take off as it did in Michigan. Numerous other locations in the Northeast and Midwest showed interest or offered attractive opportunities for auto inventors. The Michigan inventors might easily have gone to other locations. In fact, William Durant, the founder of General Motors, appeared ready to accept an offer to start his factory in Newark, New Jersey, when the offer was withdrawn. By 1904, however, Michigan was producing 42 percent of the nation's cars, a share that increased to 78 percent by 1914, thus establishing the dominance the state maintained for the next seven decades.

SOURCE: Peter Eckstein, "The Automobile In Michigan: A Case Study of Regional Development," an unpublished paper prepared for the Governor's Task Force for a Long-Term Economic Strategy for Michigan, 1984.

The economic transformation that freed people from toil in the fields and factories, enriched every region of the country, and created complex service-oriented regional economies of striking similarity is continuing. The same forces that are causing regional economies to become more similar are also creating more pronounced cleavages between urban and nonurban areas within regions. For example, the Seattle area economy is rapidly growing even as parts of Washington State, dependent on forestry, agriculture, and fishing, are stagnating.

INCREASING COMPETITIVENESS BY INDUSTRY AND REGION

While the relative share of the service sector has increased in every state, important regional differences remain. Competition is intensifying in traditional industries such as automobiles, steel, textiles, and natural resources, largely because worldwide productive capacity has expanded to meet demand. With markets in these industries no longer growing as fast as they once did, marginal differences in unit labor costs, productivity, pricing, or marketing can cause substantial shifts in market share. In industries based on new technologies, where the competitive edge depends on innovation and the ability to translate research and development quickly into marketable applications, consumer demand is driven by the availability of new products and marketing ability. Here again, marginal differences are important, especially as they affect the pace of the creation of new products, the identification of specialized consumer tastes, and the linking of research and development to marketable applications.

The economic fortunes of different regions naturally will vary according to their dependence on declining or growing industries. During the 1970s, economic forces appeared to favor the South and West. Between 1970 and 1980, total nonagricultural employment in the United States grew 30 percent. However, the East North Central States had only a 15 percent gain, whereas the Mountain States grew by 68 percent. Shifts in manufacturing employment were even more striking, in part because some states lost substantial numbers of manufacturing jobs. Total manufacturing employment in the United States increased from 19.4 million in 1970 to an historic peak of 21.0 million in 1979. Since then, manufacturing employment has edged steadily downward.[5] But the Middle Atlantic States lost 16 percent of their manufacturing jobs between 1970 and 1980, and the East North Central States lost 10 percent. During the same period, manufacturing jobs in the Mountain States increased by 57 percent and in the West South Central States by 43 percent.

Since the recessions of the early 1980s, however, the apparent advantages of the Sun Belt over the Frost Belt have faded. The New England and

---

5. *Economic Report of the President*, p. 298.

Middle Atlantic States have shown substantial economic strength, but several states in the West and South have lagged. Almost all the states in the West, South, and Midwest have had lower-than-expected revenues for fiscal 1986. In the New England and the Middle Atlantic States, however, revenues have been higher than anticipated.

Seventeen states, principally those feeling the effects of falling agricultural and oil prices, have already cut their fiscal 1986 operating budgets, an unusual occurrence in a year of national economic growth. Despite an optimistic national economic outlook, nine states — Alabama, Alaska, Kansas, Mississippi, Nebraska, North Carolina, Oklahoma, Texas, and West Virginia — are projecting lower operating budgets in fiscal 1987 because of weakening economies. Of twenty-three states that reported declining industries (mainly manufacturing and agriculture) as their most serious economic problem in 1985, there were six in the South, six in the West, five in the Midwest, and six in the Northeast.[6]

GLOBALIZATION OF THE U.S. ECONOMY

In 1950, both U.S. exports and imports were less than 5 percent of GNP. By 1980, exports had grown to 12.9 percent and imports to 11.7 percent of GNP. Exports fell to 10.2 percent of GNP in 1984, while imports remained at 11.8 percent, leaving a wide balance-of-trade deficit. These figures reflect both a growing U.S. dependence on world trade and an increased vulnerability to foreign competition.[7]

The effects of the globalization of the American economy are felt with varying degrees of intensity in different parts of the country. States that rely heavily on durable goods manufacturing have been especially hard hit by foreign competition. Southern states, which once attracted textile and shoe manufacturing from New England and the Midwest, began in the 1970s to lose jobs in those industries to foreign countries where wage rates were still lower. States that depended on extractive industries—for example, timber in Washington and Oregon, copper in Montana and Arizona—found those economic mainstays drastically diminished or lost to foreign producers. Farm states have been badly hurt by lagging exports, due in part to unfavorable exchange rates and in part to substantial increases in both U.S. and foreign farm production capacity. Most recently, the drop in oil prices has severely affected Texas, Oklahoma, Louisiana, and Alaska.

Even states strong in advanced technologies have felt the sting of foreign competition. In 1985, the Japanese captured more than 60 percent of

---

6. National Governors' Association and National Association of State Budget Officers, *Fiscal Survey of the States, 1986* (Washington, D.C.: 1986), pp. 3, 4, 5; and National Governors' Association, Center for Policy Research and Analysis, *Revitalizing State Economies*, p. 7.

---

7. *Economic Report of the President*, p. 253.

the market for 64K random-access-memory (RAM) chips. The loss of microelectronics sales abroad contributed to California's decline in exports from $4 billion in 1981 to under $3 billion in 1984.[8] The loss of semi-conductor manufacturing to Japan is an indication that being on the cutting edge of technological development is no guarantee of sustained economic advantage.

RAPID CHANGE

Change has been the essence of American economic progress. But today, the pace of change is heightened by the confluence of several important developments including: restructuring in manufacturing, the emergence of powerful new technologies, changes in the world economy, and a revolution in social values.

Consider the sudden changes that have caught states by surprise. In early 1985, Alaskan officials were planning for the possibility that oil prices might dip as low as $24 a barrel. In January 1986, Texas was still projecting the price of oil in fiscal 1987 at $24.50 a barrel. By February 1986, the price of crude oil had plummeted to below $12. In 1984, the semiconductor industry of Silicon Valley was hailed as the new engine of American economic growth; by the spring of 1985, cheap Japanese semiconductors were significantly undercutting Silicon Valley producers. In the late 1970s, Massachusetts officials began numerous programs to deal with the state's chronic unemployment, which was expected to increase because of declines in manufacturing. Today, the state is experiencing unexpectedly low unemployment and even labor shortages.

Sooner or later, moreover, the national economy is bound to turn down, and every state will be confronted with a general recession for the first time since their new economic responsibilities were widely recognized.

POTENTIAL FOR STATE ACTION

The most important implication of these changes for state policy is that the constraints or advantages associated with location, soil, access to raw materials, and even climate, although certainly not insignificant, have declined in relative importance as factors of economic production. Long-term comparative advantage among regions now has more to do with human will, skill, energy, values, costs, and organization. In a world shaped by such forces, the potential geographical scope for effective competition has been greatly enlarged.

---

8. Douglas Henton and Steven A. Waldhorn, "California: Inventing the Future through Investment and Innovation," case study prepared for the Committee for Economic Development, August 1985, p. 15.

What impact can states have on their economies in this kind of environment? In seeking guidance from past experience, we should distinguish between formal economic policy, which is explicitly designed to affect the economy, and actual economic policy, which is the sum of state actions that affect the economy whether they were intended to or not. Formal economic development policy historically has focused on efforts to attract firms to the state (see "State Economic Development Policy since 1930," page 20).

Actual state economic policy has been more significant. The nation's industrial economy could not have functioned without an education system, roads, water supply and sewage systems, ports and airports, and other services that were principally state and local government responsibilities. But such services were rarely developed as part of a conscious state economic strategy. They grew incrementally in response to political pressures and practical need. There have been a few examples of unusual state initiatives, such as the Research Triangle in North Carolina (see "Foresight in North Carolina," page 21). But the more typical experience has been a reasonably satisfactory but often tardy response to the growth engendered by market forces.

For example, California's historical economic success can be explained largely by the dynamics of the market economy fueled by spurts of activity in gold mining, agriculture, railroads, oil, entertainment, aerospace, and microelectronics. The federal government played an important role in key instances, especially in the development of the aerospace industry in southern California during and following World War II and in providing the initial demand that spawned the microelectronics industry in Silicon Valley. The state government responded to the growth engendered by these forces, providing public services, especially transportation, water supply, and education, without which economic expansion would have been stifled. There were instances of foresight by California leaders, including investment in an extensive and high-quality public higher education system.[9]

The recessions of the early 1980s prompted some of the harder-hit states to consider their economic policies more systematically. All six states that adopted formal strategic plans in 1981 and 1982 had experienced unemployment rates above the nation's average in those years. Four of the six are midwestern states.[10]

One state, Rhode Island, sought voter approval for a highly detailed economic plan with specific objectives and a precise course of action. The

---

9. Douglas Henton and Steven Waldhorn, "California: Inventing the Future," pp. 29–39.

10. National Governors' Association, *Revitalizing State Economies*, p. 5.

1,000-page *Rhode Island Greenhouse Compact,* proposed by the Rhode Island Strategic Development Commission in 1983, laid out a plan for stimulating state economic growth. In a referendum, 80 percent of state voters rejected the proposal. Surveys indicated that the voters did not understand it, were skeptical that the estimated cost of $750 million to be raised by a bond issue financed with higher taxes would yield benefits to the average

STATE ECONOMIC DEVELOPMENT POLICY SINCE 1930

- **1930 to 1950s: Industrial recruitment.** The earliest state programs aimed to attract manufacturing plants from other states. For example, in 1936, Mississippi enacted the "Balance Agriculture with Industry" program which aimed to attract low-wage manufacturing plants from the North by offering a combination of subsidies to build new plants and tax abatements for a five-year period. The federal economic development programs of the 1950s and 1960s (e.g., Area Redevelopment Act, Economic Development Administration, Appalachian Regional Commission) were similarly geared toward attracting economic activity to depressed areas. Such objectives were pursued by reducing the cost of land, labor, or capital to businesses from other locations in the belief that new plants would create jobs and bring income to a depressed area.

- **1960s: Improving equity and increasing demand through redistribution.** Federal and local programs provided subsidies to people and areas in poverty as a way both to raise incomes immediately and to increase demand to stimulate additional economic activity.

- **1970s: Economic revitalization.** Programs attempted to stimulate economic activity in depressed areas through a combination of industrial recruitment, redistribution, and private-sector investment. Greater emphasis was placed on public-private partnership and on leveraging government funds with the explicit aim of creating jobs.

- **1980s: Generative development.** Since the late 1970s, keener attention has been given to the process by which economic activity is generated within an economy. Jane Jacobs's theory on the role of cities in creating wealth and David Birch's work on the birth and death of small business have given greater weight to the notion that policy should aim not to create jobs, but to facilitate the natural dynamics of the private sector, which will create wealth and, in the process, jobs. The emphasis on entrepreneurship is a variation on this theme.[a]

a. Jane Jacobs, *The Economy of Cities* (New York: Random House, 1969); and David Birch, *The Job Generation Process* (Cambridge: 1979).

citizen, and were suspicious of the people who proposed it and would implement it.[11]

Have the new state economic initiatives undertaken since the late 1970s had an impact? It is unlikely they had much effect on economic performance in the late 1970s and early 1980s, the roots of which were firmly planted before the new wave of state activism. It is too early to tell what effect many of the initiatives are having now or will have in the future, but preliminary assessments suggest that some may be valuable.

Massachusetts offers a good case in point, because it is widely recognized as a state that has undergone a major economic transformation. The Massachusetts economic revival, as measured by job growth, is somewhat less dramatic than generally believed. Although the state's unemployment rate dropped from 12.0 percent in 1975 to 4.3 percent in 1986, employment growth has been slower than that for the United States as a whole. State programs implemented in the late 1970s and early 1980s were not responsible for stimulating the initial stages of the revival, which began as early as 1975.[12]

---

11. Thomas J. Anton and Darrell M. West, "Nothing for Something: Popular Reactions to New Industrial Policy," Brown University, 1984.

12. Ronald F. Ferguson and Helen F. Ladd, "Economic Performance and Economic Development Policy in Massachusetts," case study prepared for the Committee for Economic Development, September, 1985.

FORESIGHT IN NORTH CAROLINA

The story of the Research Triangle in North Carolina offers an unusual example of state leadership. The concept linking research and regional development in North Carolina can be traced to the chairman of the sociology department of the University of North Carolina, Howard W. Odum. Romeo H. Guest, an industrial builder and graduate of the Massachusetts Institute of Technology, gave tangible expression to the concept by proposing to promote the area bounded by Duke University in Durham, the University of North Carolina in Chapel Hill, and North Carolina State University in Raleigh, the state capital, (hence the name Research Triangle Park) as a site for industrial research laboratories. The purpose of the park was to attract firms that would draw on the knowledge and research abilities of the universities. The proposal received the enthusiastic support of Governor Luther Hodges. North Carolina in the 1950s sent missions to Massachusetts' Route 128 and California's Silicon Valley (as did Japan), which were already recognized as leading research areas. Sustained support by leaders in business, government, and the universities over the next three decades was required to turn the concept into today's reality, the Research Triangle Park.

SOURCE: Ezra Vogel, *Comeback* (New York: Simon and Schuster, 1985), pp. 243-245.

Massachusetts's initial economic revival probably can be attributed to its base in microelectronics, high-caliber universities, substantial defense contracting, and strong business services (see "Conditions for Self-Sustaining High-Technology Industrial Clusters," p. 23). Initiatives in the private sector undertaken before the 1970s may have helped to lay the base for advanced technology. For example, as early as 1946, Ralph Flanders (a founder of CED and later a U.S. senator from Vermont) organized a venture-capital fund of $4 million for the purpose of creating new businesses and jobs in New England. In the 1960s, banks and private educational institutions took special interest in the development of high technology. The continued provision of basic services by the state and local governments throughout the years of economic hardship was essential to preserving the economic base and permitting private initiatives to germinate and mature. However, these ingredients were in place and acting to generate new economic growth before the government initiatives of the late 1970s and early 1980s.

Businesses performed poorly in Massachusetts between 1967 and 1975 compared with similar industries nationwide, but a more favorable mix of high-growth industries along with an improved competitive performance in both slow and high growth industries boosted the state's economy between 1975 and 1983. Although recent economic initiatives did not cause the initial revival, some of them may have helped sustain or accelerate the momentum once the recovery was under way. These initiatives included several new quasi-public organizations, such as the Massachusetts Technology Development Corporation, the Massachusetts Industrial Finance Agency, the Community Development Finance Corporation, the Commercial Area Revitalization District Program, the Community Economic Development Assistance Corporation, and the Bay State Skills Corporation. Of broader significance is a strongly improved climate of support for business evident in state government, both in the executive and legislative branches.

The major tax-reduction initiative, Proposition $2^1/_2$, was not enacted until 1980 and therefore had no effect on the initial revival. Some observers believe, however, that, taken together with other changes in tax policy, it has had an impact in helping to persuade successful businesses to remain in the state and expand. Proposition $2^1/_2$ establishes a limit for local property taxes of $2^1/_2$ percent of the market value of taxable property and limits the annual growth in property taxes to $2^1/_2$ percent. Although the resulting savings to businesses and individuals probably did not have a substantial direct effect on economic activity, the change did signal the voters' determination to control and stabilize taxes.

CONDITIONS FOR SELF-SUSTAINING HIGH-TECHNOLOGY/INDUSTRIAL CLUSTERS

Incubator Institutions
These can be established firms or research universities. As incubators, these institutions train potential entrepreneurs and skilled manpower and expose them to the knowledge that leads to ideas for new products and businesses. In most established high-technology clusters, there are identifiable incubators, and many of the firms in the cluster have clear genealogical links.

Initial Customers
The established firms in a cluster often serve as the initial customers for new firms by subcontracting work to them and offering them consulting opportunities to smooth their cash flow. Officials of established firms also introduce new entrepreneurs to potential customers.

Models of Success
Models of success reduce the perceived risk of new ventures. Lower risk attracts more entrepreneurs into an industry than would otherwise enter. It also makes potential customers, partners, suppliers, distributors, and financiers less reluctant to enter into business relationships.

Risk Capital
Few entrepreneurs have all the money they need to finance their businesses. Hence, there must be investors and financial institutions willing to take chances on new ideas.

Management Advice
The most important sources of management advice are established firms and financiers. Financiers who work in risk finance, especially venture capitalists, have experience working with new firms and often insist on a management role during the start-up phase as a precondition to their financial participation.

Experts to Screen Ideas and Entrepreneurial Talent
Financiers and their technical advisors select people in or out of the entrepreneurial pool. Venture capital investors frequently have technical expertise as well as experience identifying people who have high potential as entrepreneurs. Because they have this expertise, they also serve as professional intermediaries for less expert investors.

SOURCE: Ronald Ferguson and Helen Ladd, "Economic Development in Massachusetts." Based on work by Roger Miller (see "Growing the Next Silicon Valley," *Harvard Business Review,* July-August 1985).

MONITORING AND EVALUATION

Experience to date, in short, demonstrates the importance of careful scrutiny in assessing the value of state economic initiatives. In any one state, some programs may be useful while others are not; the costs of programs that work may outweigh their benefits; and ambiguity as to cause and effect will require judgment.

Lacking the self-correcting mechanisms of the market economy, state governments need to monitor economic programs and evaluate their effects. Feedback is essential not only to identify programs that have out-

VIRGINIA'S CENTER FOR INNOVATIVE TECHNOLOGY (CIT)

In 1984, then Governor Charles Robb successfully promoted legislation to create an institute designed to bring the intellectual and technical assets of Virginia's universities to bear on industrial development. The debate over the purpose and accomplishment of the Center for Innovative Technology (CIT) is summarized in the following excerpts of opposing views.

A SUCCESS?

". . . has CIT done its job?
Without a doubt.

The CIT has set up engineering clinics to help medium-sized and small businesses. Programs have been designed to help firms to provide equipment to the new Continuous Beam Accelerator Facility in Newport News. The CIT has established two biotechnology, two computer-aided engineering and two materials science laboratories to assist industry-originated projects. Another new initiative will bring entrepreneurs and academics together to build up expertise in coal research, chip research, and electro-optics research.

In fact, in two years' time, the Center for Innovative Technology has initiated 166 research projects involving 70 different companies. That's not exactly shabby."

Hays T. Watkins,
Chairman of the Board of CIT

OR A FAILURE?

"Virginia's Center for Innovative Technology, originally sound in concept, is now an idea out of control.

. . . what went wrong is that a gubernatorial task force on science and technology decided it was symbolically important to 'do something' in

lived their usefulness but also to revise and retarget state actions on an ongoing basis in order to assure that their benefits are greater than their costs.

Few of the hundreds of programs undertaken by states in recent years have been subject to systematic evaluation. This is partly because they are still new, partly because of methodological difficulties, and partly because there is little incentive to undertake evaluations. It is certain, however, that in the next few years firsthand experience, informal observation, and some careful evaluation will reveal a great deal about the potential of these programs. It is also to be expected that they will be subject to political challenge (see "Virginia's Center for Innovative Technology," below).

Northern Virginia, the site of so much of Virginia's high-tech community. So the CIT was created by the General Assembly in 1984, and $50 million has been appropriated for it. This is a big item in Virginia's budget and would be enough money to pay the salaries for 25 Nobel laureates to teach in each of Virginia's engineering schools for four years.

Current plans are to construct a $30 million, nine-story building of black and white marble and gold glass near Dulles Airport. The symbolism of the center has triumphed at the expense of substance.

And that is the problem. What, in fact, is the CIT supposed to do? No one really knows.

No outside consultant was engaged to formulate the mission or purpose of the CIT. No methodology was established to determine how it should perform. And no method to monitor whether jobs are created, matching funds obtained, or research advanced — in short, whether the money is being well spent and success achieved — has ever been developed.

Worse, because the CIT is exempt from the Freedom of Information Act, the $50 million appropriated is entirely shielded from public scrutiny, creating an aura of unaccountability.

. . . a senior member of the state Senate Finance Committee, Dudley Emick, responded to reporters' questions by saying that 'the CIT's purpose was always hazy. The idea among CIT backers was: "We've got to have a flagship; don't worry about the mission." '

There are surely better, and indeed less expensive, ways to help Virginia secure its place among the high-tech centers in the United States."

J. Marshall Coleman,
former Attorney General of Virginia and Republican candidate for governor in 1981

SOURCE: *The Washington Post,* April 6, 1986.

SOURCES OF ECONOMIC INFORMATION

The following sources of economic information and analysis can be found in most states:

State agencies, including the department of economic development, financial and budget offices (where most short-term economic forecasting is done for revenue-projection purposes), planning offices, and legislative research offices. To the extent that each of the principal line agencies (e.g. transportation, education) is involved in economic affairs, they also have valuable information. One of the most underutilized sources of information is the state employment service; it has standardized industrial and occupational series and unemployment insurance administrative data.

Universities are a prime source of knowledge about the state economy. Departments of economics, business, and public affairs and special research institutes can provide assistance in foresight, analysis, monitoring, and — most neglected of all — evaluation.

Research institutes outside the university can provide useful information. For example, the Regional Economics Issues Program (REI) was organized to provide economic intelligence and policy research to the Cleveland area. REI is supported by the Cleveland Foundation and works closely with the Federal Reserve Bank of Cleveland.

Businesses, especially banks and insurance companies, are a prime source of economic data and analysis of projected changes in the economy.

Federal Reserve Banks in the various Federal Reserve Districts maintain divisions that do regional research. The New York Fed in recent years has worked directly with state and local government in New York.

The U.S. Departments of Labor and Commerce provide economic data that are useful to state policy makers.

Private consulting firms offer services in econometric forecasting, economic analysis, strategy development, and evaluation.

Theory regarding regional economic development and the role of state and local government is in flux, reflecting in part the turbulent state of economic theory generally.[13] A growing number of analysts, theoreticians, and journalists are turning their attention to the state-local arena. One can assume that revised views will result from this attention and from the added practical experience of state programs already under way. In the meantime, states will need to draw on their own experiences, analysis, and judgment in diagnosing their economic potential (see "Sources of Economic Information," page 26).

---

13. Summarizing the historical debate over economic growth policy in the United States, Herbert Stein concluded that "we do not know much with confidence about how to get more economic growth." (Herbert Stein, "Reflections on Economic Growth," *The AEI Economist*, September 1985, p. 8.) Stein cites a 1958 policy statement by CED entitled *Economic Growth in the United States: Its Past and Future* as reflecting the "center of public opinion" at that time as to the likely sources of economic growth. The list of factors included: the decentralized economic system; the amount of capital goods; the quality of business management; the quality of the labor force; the diffusion of education; the high degree of mobility; technological change and advancement; the mass market and advertising; consumer credit; savings and income; and the growth of the money supply.

One of the principal staff members who worked on that policy statement, Edward F. Denison, proceeded to quantify the most important of these factors. In the most recent update of his analysis of the sources of economic growth, Denison concluded that percentage contributions to actual growth of national income from 1929-78 were: labor (except education), 32; education per worker, 14; capital, 19; advances in knowledge, 28; improved resource allocation, 8; and economies of scale, 9. Other factors such as regulation detracted 9 percent from overall growth. Denison also concluded that, after 1973, "growth rates of both potential and actual output were much reduced and the previous persistent increase in output per person employed had stalled." This slowdown in growth, Denison found, continued for more than a decade and showed no sign of re-acceleration. (Edward F. Denison, *Trends in American Economic Growth, 1929–82* (Washington, D.C.: The Brookings Institution, 1985), p. 30.)

Chapter 3

Vision: Setting Direction

LOUISIANA
MAINE
MARYLAND
MASSACHUSETTS
MICHIGAN
MINNESOTA
MISSISSIPPI
MISSOURI

Vision is required to harness long-term forces in the service of the state's economic goals. An effective vision can give direction and cohesion to specific government actions and help avoid the pitfalls and tempting quick-fixes that can undermine long-term performance.

The vision will, of course, vary for each state depending on its circumstances and the desires of its citizens. All the states, however, are similar enough that their visions are likely to share certain common elements. Many states, for example, might subscribe to the following general goals:

- jobs, higher incomes, and low unemployment
- higher gross state product and wealth
- opportunity for all to be part of the state's economic potential
- stability that minimizes the extremes in cyclical performance
- diversity to reduce dependence on a few industries
- geographic balance among parts of the state
- equity in the distribution of economic benefits among all segments of society

In choosing goals, leaders must ask whether state government is involving itself unduly in the economy. Economic goals cannot be dissociated from other state goals, because economic pursuits are not ends in themselves, but means to provide the necessities of life and the opportunities for personal and civic development. An economic vision should be part of a broader vision that encompasses the personal, family, cultural, environmental, civic, and spiritual dimensions of a state that seeks to be as great as it is capable of being.

Such a vision can provide a constructive focus for long-term mutual effort. It does not ignore tough political choices; it confronts them in the selection of actions that are most in keeping with the community-held vision.

FOSTERING A VITAL PRIVATE SECTOR

Central to a state's vision of the economic future should be a vital, market-driven private sector. A free market permits consumers to choose the products and services they want at competitive prices. It requires producers to provide what consumers want and to compete to keep quality high and prices low. Market incentives also provide opportunity for individuals and businesses to take risks and to use their imagination, knowledge, skills, energy, capital, and technology — the basic stocks of wealth-creating capability — to create new products and services that people want or to improve on those already being provided.

It is through such market dynamics that value is created. And without the creation of value there will be no enduring jobs. Policies that aim to create "instant jobs" that do not create value, on the other hand, are self-defeating in the long run.

A free market also permits the economy to find its own way into the future through thousands of individual consumer choices and producer initiatives. Producers who take risks and offer new, better, or cheaper products create value, and they are rewarded for it. Producers who cannot match that performance must turn their energies and resources to pursuits in which they are competitive or else go out of business.

Time and again, a vigorous, market-driven private sector has demonstrated its ability not only to assure that existing stocks of wealth-creating capability are efficiently used and replenished, but also to change fundamentally the mix of stocks when conditions permit or require it. Government is no passive bystander in this process. Government is instrumental in determining economic value through the political system, and it contributes critically to the foundations on which the private sector depends.

Years of economic success lulled Americans into thinking of economic development in relatively static terms. Signs of vulnerability in recent years have heightened awareness of the dynamic nature of the economy, and hence, of the importance of change and adjustment in achieving economic progress. That is one reason for the renewed interest in entrepreneurship.

Entrepreneurs are agents of change. They seek out opportunities to increase value to themselves and others and to mobilize the resources needed to turn opportunity into tangible reality. They are creative in doing so, eschewing conventional wisdom when it obstructs rather than guides productive change. The image of an entrepreneur as an inventor or a businessman is only partly correct. An entrepreneur may be anyone who, in the classical economic meaning of the word, puts resources to a more highly valued use. This can occur in both the public and the private sectors. In CED's 1982 policy statement *Public-Private Partnership: An Opportunity for Urban Communities,* we emphasized the importance of the *civic entrepreneur,* a leader from either the public or the private sector who "envisions an opportunity where others see problems, has a sense of how to get from here to there, and is committed to working until that opportunity is fulfilled."[1]

The state's impact on the private sector is typically expressed in terms of its business climate, which is often vaguely defined. The conventional definition emphasizes constraints on business such as labor, land, utility costs, taxes, and regulation. Another definition stresses the presence of resources that support business, including skilled labor, adequate suppliers, accessible markets, good infrastructure, available capital, high quality of life, and a supportive attitude.

Business climate can also vary for types of firms. The Alexander Grant index, for example, measures twenty-three factors, most of which are geared toward the cost of locating a manufacturing plant in the state.[2] The magazine *Inc.* compiles an index that attempts to assess the environment for growing small business and entrepreneurial firms.[3] The two indexes can yield dramatically different results. For example, in 1984, Mississippi was ranked sixth by Alexander Grant and forty-ninth by *Inc.* In 1982, California was ranked twenty-sixth by Alexander Grant and second by *Inc.*

In practice, all businesses seek a combination of both minimum constraints and maximum supports. The mix varies according to the nature and size of the business and whether it is seeking to start up, expand, or relocate.

Cost reduction and the provision of supportive resources are not necessarily mutually exclusive. **A state's priorities in creating a vital private sector should be both to facilitate change and to provide supports that are important to business in general.**

FACILITATING CHANGE

The most important conflict in the economy is between the past and the future. Policies that inhibit change may seem appealing and may enjoy

---

1. Committee for Economic Development, *Public-Private Partnership: An Opportunity for Urban Communities* (New York: 1982), p. 24.

2. Alexander Grant & Company, *The sixth annual study of General Manufacturing Climates of the Forty-eight Contiguous States of America* (Washington, D.C.: June 1985), pp. 30-35.

3. Nell Margolis, "INC's Fifth Annual Report on the States," *Inc.*, vol. 7 (October 1985), pp. 92-93.

strong political support from those who benefit from the status quo, but they are likely to be counterproductive in the long run.

For example, business decisions to close plants, transfer work, or automate are necessary if corporations are to remain competitive and protect the long-term interests of their shareholders and employees. Intrusion on this essential flexibility will do more than hurt the company; it can increase unemployment and diminish contributions to the vitality of the economy as a whole.

On the other hand, positive steps can be taken to ease the adjustment of workers to other employment and to help communities compensate for a reduction in their tax base. Efforts to assist in modernization or the salvaging of parts of the businesses that have economic potential may be worthwhile.[4] Thirteen states, including those hardest hit with plant closings, have targeted programs to encourage the modernization, restructuring, or diversification of mature firms. Two of these states have established funds to finance the transfer of ownership, and nine assist employees who wish to purchase firms to forestall a plant closing. State governments need to look carefully at their laws, regulations, and programs to ascertain whether any are handicapping the ability of citizens or businesses to adjust to change.

States that have been the most successful in buffering their citizens against the effects of cyclical economic downturns in the past may face their most difficult challenge in adjusting to long-term structural change. Those that have enjoyed the greatest economic success in the past may be the least likely to feel the need to change or may have created the most impenetrable barriers against change. States in the Northeast and Midwest that enacted generous benefit programs during the growth years of the 1960s found that those programs inhibited workers from seeking retraining or new employment, created heavy tax burdens for existing businesses, and impeded the creation of potential new businesses. States in the South and West that relied heavily on natural resources to finance state government are now discovering that squeezed budgets make it difficult to sustain the public services required to support economic activity and facilitate the transition to new, more diverse industries.

BUILDING ECONOMIC FOUNDATIONS

Perhaps the most important role for states is to invest in the foundations on which the economy needs to grow, adapt, and compete. These foundations include the following:

- **a capable and motivated work force** that is well educated and sup-

---

4. National Governors' Association, *Revitalizing State Economies*, p. 9.

ported by a human resource system that facilitates and assists in finding employment

- **sound physical infrastructure,** including transportation, communications, energy, water supply, and waste management

- **well-managed natural resources** for current and future use and development

- **universities and other research and development institutions** that are involved in the development, dissemination, and market applications of knowledge and technology

- **a system of regulation, capital, and technical assistance** that encourages enterprise development

- **a quality of life** that is attractive to employees and their families

- **fiscal stability** characterized by reasonable tax rates and prudent spending policy

States have major responsibilities for each of these foundations, and those responsibilities provide the focus for practical action. (For a detailed discussion, see Chapter 4.) In some cases, the task is to repair foundations that have been permitted to deteriorate. This is especially true for education and physical infrastructure. The emerging economy will require new foundations and some major renovation of old foundations. For example, today greater attention must be given to the development and application of knowledge and technology. The quality of life is not only an important factor in attracting and retaining business, but also the source of important economic ventures in tourism and recreation. Some natural resources such as land and water will be major economic assets.

In shaping their foundations to be compatible with emerging economic forces, states inescapably will make judgments about the future nature of the economy. On some of these judgments, there will be little disagreement. No one disputes the need for strong education as a valuable economic asset. Everyone agrees that roads are important. But as state policies move farther away from the traditional foundations toward specific technologies, industries, or firms, the judgments become subject to greater uncertainty, controversy, and error.

Even in such areas as education and transportation, where everyone agrees the state has a role, judgments about the future are not so obvious, and choices bias the state's economy in one direction or another. For example, what constitutes a strong education — technical skills, computer training, problem-solving abilities, abstract reasoning, English literacy, habits of personal discipline? The decisions the state makes about how to educate its children will strongly influence the character of its work force and its ability to compete in the economy of the future. To what extent should roads receive priority over railroads, ports, airports, mass transit, or telecommunication networks that may supplant some of the demand for transportation? The kind of transportation the state supports could strongly influence the economic potential of different firms and industries.

In areas where there is even less experience, judgments are subject to even greater uncertainty and controversy. The role of states in research and development falls squarely in this category. Numerous states are sponsoring new research and development institutions or partnerships among universities and businesses that not only assume that research and development is economically important (a widely accepted view that involves assumptions about the economy of the future), but more pointedly target particular areas of research and methods of linking research and market development. Frequently, the targeted area is related to some economic asset of the state. Michigan, for example, is sponsoring institutes to develop robotics for application to its durable goods manufacturing and to develop biotechnology related to its forestry and agriculture industries. Colorado has established the Colorado Advanced Technology Institute to encourage basic and applied research through Centers for Excellence in such fields as advanced materials, microelectronics, and telecommunications. Do such plans involve the states unduly in attempting to pick the industries or technologies

THE HIGH-TECH RACE

States are vying to attract high-technology industries for their growth, high value added, and job-generating potential. But caution is in order.

There is widespread disagreement over the definition of high tech. Narrowly defined high-tech industries such as microelectronics, fiber optics, genetic engineering, and high strength ceramics are projected to generate only about five percent of new jobs over the next ten years. Broader definitions are based variously on a firm's proportion of research and development expenditures or share of technology-oriented job titles. They encompass industries such as soaps, cleaners, and toilet preparations; tires and inner tubes; and petroleum refining.

A more meaningful definition of high tech is the application of new knowledge in any industry to either product, process, or service, resulting in a new market offering that is clearly differentiated on a global basis. Thus, the steel, financial services, and health industries can and should be thought of as *high tech*. By this definition, nearly all industries and all regions can reap the benefits of a high-tech approach to growth and competitiveness.

of the future, or do they reflect a reasonable effort to prepare the state to be competitive in the future economy?*

To a large extent, these are situational questions that require consideration of specific proposals and their costs, potential impact, and level of risk that can be addressed only in a particular economic, fiscal, and political context. **We believe the appropriate degree of state government involvement must be addressed on a state-by-state, issue-by-issue basis and must also be subject to a stringent test of costs, benefits, and potential market distortion.**

It would be foolhardy, for example, for a state to commit major funding for the development of an exotic technology that is unrelated to the state's economic base and has little prospect of economic return. On the other hand, it may be a prudent hedging of bets and intelligent experimentation for a state to appropriate affordable sums to develop its capability in technologies that may be important to key sectors of its economy. In general, the more specialized a state economy or the more vulnerable the industries on which it depends, the more justifiable its concern with specific resources, technologies, industries, and firms because its vulnerability is greater and its opportunities for adjustment are fewer. That does not justify special treatment to compensate for the failure of firms to adjust to market forces, but it does mean the state has a practical need to consider its relatively higher degree of vulnerability.

Whatever the nature of the state economy, the further removed from basic foundations and generic programs a proposed policy is, and the closer that policy moves toward favoring specific technologies, industries, or firms, the greater the danger that it will reflect nothing more than wishful thinking at best or political pork-barreling at worst.

One of the reasons such choices are better left to the private sector is that the market provides an efficient self-correcting mechanism for failure that the public sector lacks. Private ventures that fail to prove themselves financially viable will go out of business. In contrast, government sponsored ventures will continue even if unsuccessful, so long as their supporters can mobilize the political clout to sustain their funding through the state budget. Once established, even so seemingly worthy a venture as a research institute will develop an immediate political constituency that will be interested in continuing the institute even if it fails to accomplish its public purpose. That constituency will include those who proposed it and wish to avoid the embarrassment of failure, employees and contractors whose compensation depends on it, affiliated organizations that may benefit from its product at little or no cost, and the region or municipality in which it is located.

Even in those instances where new ventures can be justified as a prudent risk with potential for genuine economic gain, steps should be taken

---

*See memorandum by RALPH E. BAILEY (page 88).

at the beginning to provide for public accountability. This can be accomplished by requiring a clear statement of purpose, establishing the criteria by which the venture will be judged, determining who will monitor and evaluate its performance, and setting a specific time for the evaluation.

The ultimate discipline in determining the real value of actions to the state's economy is that the state itself will reap the benefit or bear the loss. If that is not sufficient incentive to caution state leaders and citizens against frivolous or narrowly self-serving actions, they should also consider that in today's competitive environment the adverse effects of actions harmful to the state's economy can be magnified many times as competitors move to seize the advantage.

DEALING PRAGMATICALLY WITH COMPETITIVE CHALLENGES

The competitive challenge is complicated when the governments of other states and nations try to give their home industries an advantage. Even states with strong high-technology bases are concerned about their vulnerability, not just to aggressive private competitors, but also to aggressive government policies in competing states or nations.

Californians are alarmed that their leadership in microelectronics is being challenged by foreign competition and have had to contend with what the Department of Commerce has now ruled was unfair dumping of semiconductors in the American market by Japanese firms. University and business leaders in Massachusetts are asking whether that state's high-technology economy is vulnerable to the Japanese challenge. Their concern is heightened by the knowledge that specialized economies are vulnerable to rapidly changing economic forces and to the policies of aggressive foreign business.

The best economic weapon to deal with the outside competitive challenge is a vital private sector honed to a competitive edge by world market forces. The approaches we have outlined for fostering a vital private sector, facilitating change, and building economic foundations therefore also form the basis for an effective strategy to deal with outside competition.

States cannot ignore the reality of outside competitive challenges, but they need to respond pragmatically, distinguishing among different types of actions and countering competition in ways appropriate to the specific problem without undermining their long-term competitive strength or the free market environment. Competing jurisdictions may at times offer incentives to employers that may be uneconomical in the long run but are nonetheless attractive to business in the short run, especially in those fields thought to have important growth potential. To leaders of the state that is losing out to such inducements, theoretical arguments about free trade, comparative advantage, or market forces can seem less important than the very practical questions they face about lost jobs and the future of their economies. It is understandable that a state's leaders caught in these circumstances might try to match those incentives being proposed elsewhere. Such action-reaction, beggar-thy-neighbor tactics ought to be minimized. But sometimes states are pressed to act. **When that happens, states would be well advised to keep their countermeasures temporary, as generic as possible, and of a type that does not seriously distort the rest of the state economy.** States should also anticipate such threats and act to strengthen the economic sectors at risk.

Unfortunately, many states continue to view their competitive positions principally in terms of their ability to attract business from outside the state. Targeted financial incentives used to induce firms to relocate distort the market, are unlikely to yield benefits that outweigh their costs, provoke similar measures from other states that yield a net loss all around, and rarely are the deciding factor in location selection. Furthermore, they are of little economic consequence even when successful because relocation represents only a small fraction of economic growth in any given state. But perhaps most important, preoccupation with recruitment distracts from the central issue of competitiveness: how to build a strong economy *from within* that can compete on a global scale.*

We believe that state recruitment efforts should focus on providing accurate and useful information to business on the nature of the state economy, the strength of its foundations, and worthwhile location opportunities; not on the provision of financial incentives. It is important for states to make sure that businesses have accurate information about the economy because ignorance or misinformation, such as an unfair anti-business image, may cause businesses to make uninformed location decisions. It is also a useful service to business to provide practical information about location opportunities. Financial subsidies, however, are rarely a significant concern in wise business-location decisions and usually amount to little more than a government giveaway and burden on taxpayers, including corporate taxpayers forced to subsidize their competitors.

States should establish policies conducive to strong economic performance and competitive position. This can best be done by creating an environment conducive to enterprise in general, not by policies designed to benefit one firm at the expense of another. It will be to a state's long-run economic disadvantage to inhibit either the adjustments that could increase the competitiveness of existing industry or the emergence of new industries, services and firms that could provide future economic growth.

We do not subscribe to the notion that so-called export or trade industries deserve special treatment from state governments. Industries that produce substitutes for imported goods and services or that serve local needs which would otherwise have to be met with imports can be just as important

---

*See memorandum by FRANKLIN A. LINDSAY (page 89).

as those whose products are traded outside the state. However, that does not mean states should ignore the reality that they will need to produce goods and services of value to others if they are to generate revenue to import the things they need. This reality should be confronted not by subsidizing potential export industries, but by creating a climate in which industries with export potential can flourish. There may be justification for states to help businesses, especially small businesses, identify export opportunities and develop markets outside the state but such activities should be limited to those which the private sector demonstrably cannot undertake on its own.

ENHANCING REGIONAL ECONOMIES

States are political jurisdictions whose boundaries rarely correspond to de facto economic regions. State governments possess significant powers to affect the economic regions they encompass or of which they form a part. For example, every time a state chooses a location for a government office, decides where to build a highway, hospital, university, or community college, or agrees to finance a port, airport, or other transportation, commercial, or communications facility, it invariably affects the economies of particular regions.

Dynamic and entrepreneurial urban economies are themselves important economic assets. For example, Alaska's economy is based on natural resources. But the city of Anchorage has grown in a decade from a small town that imported almost everything to a city of 250,000 that produces paint, petroleum, furniture, clothing, and a range of home-based legal, financial, engineering, printing, medical, and business services.

Some regions suffer acute economic distress. Many natural resource-based rural economies and the cores of many urban areas are afflicted with problems that can affect not only the people and businesses in those areas, but the entire state as well.

Some states have attempted to recognize their impact on regional economic conditions. Massachusetts has adopted a policy of geographic targeting in an attempt to revitalize distressed older cities and to relieve suburban congestion (see Geographic Targeting in Massachusetts, page 38). California's *Master Plan for Higher Education* consciously spread colleges and universities over 134 campuses in communities throughout the state. Several states, including Massachusetts, Pennsylvania, Michigan, and North Carolina, are creating regional centers for research, technology application, or other economic specialities. New Hampshire has organized its community college system so as to shift training resources to meet the changing needs in different regions of the state. Eleven states acknowledge formally targeting geographic areas in their economic development strategies.[5] "In two other projects, the impacts of technology are being studied. Under the auspices of the Council of State Planning Agencies and the leadership of Governor Kerrey of Nebraska, one project is analyzing the impacts of the revolution in telecommunications technology on state regulatory and nonregulatory policies. In the other project, the Midwestern Technology Development Institute, supported by ten state governors, is studying the regional impacts of the revolution in high technology."

A vision for the state should be a blending of concerns for its regions.

---

5. National Governors' Association, *Revitalizing State Economies*, pp. 5-6.

GEOGRAPHIC TARGETING IN MASSACHUSETTS

The most ambitious state program of geographic targeting to date has been in Massachusetts, which in 1975 established a policy of steering growth toward the older industrial cities. The policy grew out of an extensive consensus-building effort involving over 5,000 citizens in Local Growth Policy Committees in 330 of the state's 351 cities and towns.

What state officials developed was not so much a comprehensive plan for the geographic distribution of new investment as a mode of operation that emphasized "employing the state's resources in any way state officials could think of to revitalize the urban center." For example, a state program provided $10 million in state funds to the Lowell Heritage Park. This money was used along with a much larger grant from the federal government to develop the park, which highlights early textile manufacturing in the city as a tourist attraction and component of the city's economic revitalization. Similar Heritage Parks have since been established throughout the state.

Through an executive order, Governor Michael Dukakis required all moves and expansions of state office facilities to be in existing structures in target cities. The state's Office of Federal State Relations also persuaded the Federal Urban Systems Highway Program to make improvements in downtown streets and sidewalks and beautification, rather than just improving traffic flows. Federal grants for highways and sewers were steered toward the targeted areas. Most of these actions required no change in state law. One of the few laws enacted, the Commercial Area Revitalization District Act, restricted the commercial use of industrial development bonds to specially designated commercial revitalization districts.

While there is insufficient evidence to conclude that geographic targeting has contributed to the aggregate performance of the state economy, it has helped revitalize distressed areas. Whether that benefit justifies the costs entailed remains an open question.

SOURCE: Ronald F. Ferguson and Helen F. Ladd, "Economic Performance and Economic Development Policy in Massachusetts," case study prepared for the Committee for Economic Development, September, 1985.

Chapter 4

Action: Getting There

A vision is useful only to the extent that it is translated into *tangible* and *completable* actions. The foundations discussed in Chapter 2 provide a useful framework for considering the many state actions that have economic impact. Figure 1, page 40, lists the principal state responsibilities associated with each of those foundations. The figures in Appendix B offer a more detailed breakdown of those responsibilities and their economic implications.

At any given time, a wide array of seemingly unconnected actions may be on the priority list of state leaders. For example, a list of actions identified by public- and private-sector leaders in Massachusetts in February 1986 includes items that touch on all the state economic foundations (see "An Action Agenda in Massachusetts," page 41). Such priorities, of course, will change as some problems are solved and others arise.

The foundation framework can help leaders to see how such issues relate to one another so that energy can be focused and efforts better coordinated. It can also help to identify state actions that are not generally considered part of an economic strategy but that nonetheless have important economic consequences.

This chapter discusses the types of actions that fall within the foundation framework. In doing so, we aim to suggest an approach to creating agendas for action rather than making specific suggestions for actions to be taken, for that is clearly a matter for each state to determine.

HUMAN RESOURCES

The skill, motivation, and adaptability of the work force are strongly influenced by state action. The vital role played by public education in preparing new workers has been recognized by at least twenty states, which have undertaken education initiatives in order to improve their economies.[1]

---

1. National Governors' Association, *Revitalizing State Economies*, p. 3.

FIGURE 1
Areas of State Government Action that Affect Economic Foundations

Work Force	Physical Infrastructure	Natural Resources	Knowledge and Technology
Primary and secondary education	Transportation	Land	Information dissemination
Higher education	Water supply and sewage	Water	Public universities
Labor market adjustment	Waste management	Air	Research and development support
Employment security	Communication regulation	Agriculture	Linkages among universities, research, and business
Health	Energy regulation	Minerals	
Human services	Housing	Forests	
Labor relations		Wildlife	

Enterprise Development	Quality of Life		Fiscal Management
Promotion to attract investment	Management of the physical environment		General taxes
Financial incentives to business	Regulation of private goods and services		Business taxes and fees
Technical assistance to business	Amenities		Expenditures for public services
Regulation and involvement in capital market	Community		Debt
Regulation of business			Other costs
Export promotion			

Preparation in primary and secondary schools establishes the basic skills for getting a job, training for a job, or seeking higher education, which will, in turn, lead to a job. CED recently recommended ways to improve primary and secondary education in the policy statement **Investing in Our Children: Business and the Public Schools.** Higher education is increasingly important in preparing people for the growing number of knowledge-based occupations.

Training beyond formal education is required to keep workers up-to-date with technological change and the skill needs of industry. Retraining is necessary for workers to update job skills or to switch jobs when they are displaced due to business contraction, automation, or relocation. People are not always easily matched with jobs for which they are best suited. Some cannot find work; others accept jobs that do not fully use their capabilities. Typically, the state government provides many types and levels of assistance to help meet these needs: vocational training, unemployment compensation, employment services. But such services often are not coor-

AN ACTION AGENDA IN MASSACHUSETTS

Early in 1986, a meeting convened by Jobs for Massachusetts, a group of top-level public- and private-sector leaders including the governor, identified the priority actions needed to continue the state's successful economic development. The group's list included:

- Strengthen higher education, both public and private.
- Expand skills training, such as through increased funding of the Bay State Skills Corporation.
- Increase private-sector participation on the board of regents and strengthen the community college system.
- Improve access to the airport with a third harbor tunnel, or find a site for a new airport.
- Find six new solid waste disposal sites.
- Develop a means of disposing of hazardous waste.
- Build energy capacity and efficiency.
- Develop the state's base in biotechnology.
- Cut down on the permits required to start a business.
- Reform state tort law.
- Reduce health care costs; consider a "maloccurrence" system.
- Create opportunity for all people and regions of the state.

dinated to help people develop and use their skills to greatest effect, or to match an employer's need with a worker's skills and potential.

In the workplace, relationships between employees and employers are affected by laws and regulations governing unions, civil rights, safety, and health. Labor productivity and the cost to employers of pending medical insurance are affected by the state through the regulation of health care.

Programs to help nontraditional workers (i.e., minorities, youth, the elderly, the disadvantaged, refugees) develop their skills and find employment have usually been justified on equity grounds. But there is also a strong economic argument for making full use of all human potential, both to reduce the burden on government support programs and to supply skilled workers in labor shortage areas. The many state programs that have shifted from traditional welfare programs toward a strategy of investing in people's employment potential, such as Massachusetts' Employment and Training program, reflect this view.

The state may be actively involved with each of these elements (see Appendix B, Figure B-1). However, it is equally important that states recognize the way in which these programs affect one another, and, in turn, operate as part of a broader education, training, compensation, and job search network.

Following are some examples of state efforts to integrate human resources and economic development.

- Illinois has linked its employment, training, and economic development programs in state-designated enterprise zones. The fund established from state and federal resources trains dislocated workers for employment in any of the state's twenty zones. Funds may be used for classroom or on-the-job training.

- Vermont has created a Job Skills Cabinet to improve coordinating state employment, training, and economic development assistance. One approach has been the sponsorship of Regional Connection Workshops where government, business, and civic organizations from substate regional economies have come together to cooperate in their training and employment efforts.

- California has established a workforce program that combines traditional welfare programs, such as Aid to Families with Dependent Children, and Job Training Partnership Act (JTPA) programs to focus on preparing people for real labor-market needs.

- In Nebraska, a state Department of Labor employee is assigned to the Department of Economic Development to market and package comprehensive training funds for local officials and businesses. Funding decisions can be made quickly because the program manager has the authority to commit resources.

- Missouri has attempted a more integrated approach to customized training by combining federal and state funds to support projects for training dislocated workers. This means that the state's employment agency is working with the economic development agency to provide comprehensive customized training.

- Florida has created the Florida Integrated Community Development Program. State Community Development Block Grant economic development projects are integrated with state employment, training, and growth-management programs.

PHYSICAL INFRASTRUCTURE

The traditional elements of infrastructure — transportation, water supply, sewage disposal, housing, communication, energy distribution — are essential in the contemporary economy (listed in Appendix B, Figure B-2). Bridges, for example, because of their maintenance costs, can no longer be taken for granted. Airports are valued for their importance to business travel and increasingly as a basic amenity. Railroads that were once thought uneconomical have again become valued assets in many areas. New technologies are transforming some conventional ideas of infrastructure. For example, advanced telecommunications networks have become critical to many communities.

Alarm over the so-called infrastructure crisis in the nation has brought well-deserved attention to the importance of quality, capacity, access, and cost of physical infrastructure to economic performance. However, exaggerations of the problem can obscure the real economic connection. Public works improvements are no guarantee of better economic performance. In fact, some improvements may be wasteful if they create underutilized capacity or generate excessive overhead costs. Moreover, new infrastructure can merely shift economic activity from one community to another without contributing to the entire economy's development.

Infrastructure decisions can affect economic performance in several ways.

- Expanded transportation, water supply, and waste systems are needed to accommodate growth.

- Inadequate maintenance of existing systems can interrupt economic activity or increase its costs.

- Underutilized capacity offers opportunities for economic growth at low additional cost but creates high operating costs for present users.
- Specific infrastructure improvements may be required in order for particular projects to proceed.
- The cost of infrastructure expansion, maintenance, and operation can constitute an important cost of doing business.

The connection between physical infrastructure and economic development should be assessed not just in terms of aggregate expenditures but also with respect to the impact of individual projects. This is frequently best determined at the local level, where the costs for alternative projects and their importance to the local economy can be more accurately evaluated.

Examples of efforts to improve state and local infrastructure include the following:

- Washington State's Public Works Trust Fund makes loans to local jurisdictions for the repair, replacement, and reconstruction of existing systems based on a public works inventory. To qualify, local jurisdictions must impose a dedicated excise tax for capital purposes and have in place a local long-term capital financing plan.
- The Mississippi Business Investment Program provides below-market rate loans to local communities on a matching basis (with government or private-sector participation) for public capital investments to support new growth industries.
- The New Jersey Waste Water Treatment Trust Fund was created to finance local projects starting in 1987. The Trust Fund is capitalized by state bonds and will issue its own revenue bond in support of loans to localities for waste water treatment facilities.

NATURAL RESOURCES

Historically, natural resources have been among the most important determinants of economic development. Agricultural economies have depended on good soil and climate; manufacturing-based economies on accessible materials and low-cost energy. Sufficient access to clean water has been a prerequisite for economic activity. Figure B-3 of Appendix B shows the principal elements of state natural resource management.

The national economy's transition to knowledge- and service-based industries has diminished the relative value of some natural resources, with strong repercussions in states that have depended on them in the past. Traditional copper-mining states such as Montana and Arizona have undergone major adjustments as domestic copper production has declined. The farm states, especially Iowa, Nebraska, and Kansas, are suffering serious economic problems caused by falling farm prices, the drop in farm exports, overextended debt, and reductions in federal subsidy payments. The average value of farmland in Nebraska dropped 46 percent between 1981 and 1985. During the first seven months of 1985, 62 percent of the banks that failed in the United States were agricultural banks.[2] Plummeting oil prices not only hurt the oil-producing states (Texas, Louisiana, Oklahoma, and Alaska) but also have affected the states that produce other energy resources, such as natural gas (Wyoming) and coal (West Virginia, Kentucky, and Ohio).

In the meantime, other natural resources, especially land and water, are taking on growing importance for virtually all states. The state government plays a major role in the construction and development of water supply, both directly and through its regulatory and financing authority over local governments. The state's role in the regulation of land use, again both directly and through its impact on the powers of local governments, is of growing importance as urban areas grow beyond local government boundaries and greater pressures are placed on important natural resources such as estuaries and agricultural land.

Examples of state natural resource initiatives include the following:

- Arizona enacted a Groundwater Management Act in 1980 to provide for bringing water from the Colorado River and to manage the growing demands for ground water that were threatening to disrupt the state's economic development of its desert environment.

- Montana is one of seven states with a natural resource severance tax. Uses for the receipts of this fund include alternative energy research, park acquisition, cultural preservation, renewable-resource development, county and local land-use planning, and conservation districts.

- California has adopted a comprehensive package of investment funds to enhance the long-term productivity of the state's natural resources. Priority initiatives include reforestation, improved forest productivity, geothermal energy development, salmon restoration, and desalinization of irrigation runoff.[3]

---

2. U.S. General Accounting Office, *Financial Condition of American Agriculture,* Report No. GAO/RCED 89-09.

---

3. William E. Nothdurft, *Renewing America: Natural Resource Assets and State Economic Development* (Washington, D.C.: The Council of State Planning Agencies, 1984), p. 115.

KNOWLEDGE AND TECHNOLOGY

Today's advanced technology is different from that of the past. Disciplines are increasingly specialized. The lines between basic and applied research have become blurred and in some cases have been eliminated completely. As one observer has described the situation: "One cannot use Edisonian techniques — '99% perspiration and 1% inspiration' — to create monoclonal antibodies, or a bacterium carrying a human gene, or molecular beam epitaxy for layering semiconductors."[4]

There are important differences in the rate of technological applications among various scientific fields. In the life sciences, for example, the time required to move from basic research to the development of usable products may be very long. But in microelectronics, where the line between research and development has all but disappeared, new discoveries may lead to almost immediate applications, and innovation in commercial products may redefine the boundaries of basic research.

The states view knowledge and technology as economically important in assisting existing business, developing employment opportunities, creating new businesses, and attracting the branches and headquarters of out-of-state firms. Universities, many of which are state-supported, play a key role both because they provide specific services and because a good university system is considered a general attraction to firms. However, many states have initiated efforts that go beyond traditional university functions.

- The Georgia Institute of Technology has adapted the land grant college agriculture extension model in establishing twelve industrial stations throughout the state.

- The Pennsylvania Technology Assistance Program emphasizes the dissemination of technology through a network of transfer agents, a library-based computer information system, and continuing education.

- In Iowa, a state less well-known for the promotion of advanced technologies, the governor's High Technology Task Force recommended increasing state outlays for research and establishing several research and development centers near research universities in the state as part of an overall plan to accelerate economic development.

- The Arkansas Science and Technology Authority was created in 1983 to promote the establishment of high technology industries and to sup-

---

4. Frank Press, in *The Economics of Amenity: Community Futures and the Quality of Life,* by Robert H. McNulty, Dorothy R. Jacobson, and R. Leo Penne (Washington, D.C.: Partners in Livable Places, 1985), pp. 68, 83-84, and 430.

port basic and applied research in Arkansas universities. It is authorized to make seed capital investments in high tech companies, provide funding for basic and applied research, and establish incubator facilities under the auspices of Arkansas colleges and universities.

- Maine has established the Maine Science and Technology Board, a private, nonprofit agency with members from business, labor, education, and government appointed by the governor. The Board identified needs for technology development in the state, and research centers have been established at the University of Maine in support of natural resource industries.

Critical to the state's role in developing its knowledge and technology base is the relationship between state government, universities, and industry. This relationship is discussed in Chapter 6.

ENTERPRISE DEVELOPMENT

The area most commonly associated with state economic policy is that combination of government actions — principally promotional information, financing, technical assistance, and regulation — that is thought to affect most directly the location and expansion decisions of individual businesses. Techniques drawn from each of these areas have been used for many years by state governments in conventional development programs designed to attract out-of-state firms. Incentives range from simple promotional literature describing the state's business environment and amenities to elaborate packages of tax breaks, subsidies, training stipends, and actions to facilitate licensing and zoning procedures.

As state development efforts have expanded beyond recruitment to include the creation, expansion, and retention of businesses within the state, many of the same techniques have been employed, and numerous new techniques have been added. Unfortunately, the simultaneous rapid expansion of targeting techniques has created confusion as to the aims of enterprise development policy and increased the possibility that programs may be ineffective or counterproductive. For example, the sudden growth in programs for small business, prompted in part by David Birch's research on the relationship between small business and job generation, may have caused several important points to have been overlooked. One point that was overlooked is that it is not small businesses so much as new and expanding businesses that account for new jobs.[5] A second is that many small businesses grow by receiving outsourcing contracts from big busi-

---

5. Roger J. Vaughan, Robert Pollard, and Barbara Dyer, *The Wealth of States*, pp. 40-41.

ness. A third is that the research on job generation is relatively new and confined largely to the 1970s. The economic dynamics that accounted for job generation by firms during that period may not apply in all periods or stages of economic development.

The point is not that small business is unimportant. It is very important and should be strongly encouraged. Neither is it that new business is necessarily more important than small business, nor that expanding business is more important than new business. However, in correcting for an overemphasis on attracting out-of-state businesses in the past, states should not assume that they can target their efforts on any one type of business activity in the future. The numerous actions by state government that directly affect business operations should be regularly reviewed to assure that they are enhancing the ability of business enterprise in all stages of development to change and grow in response to market forces.

A multitude of programs now aims to assist the start-up and expansion of new businesses through the provision of seed capital, product development, and expansion financing. For example:

- The **Indiana Community Business Credit Corporation** was established by the Indiana legislature as a for-profit entity to provide a pool of credit so that Indiana member banks, through loan participations, could reduce their risks in lending to new or rapidly growing small business; and

- The **Connecticut Product Development Corporation (CPDC)** has been in operation for more than a decade. CPDC typically provides existing manufacturers with financing of up to 60 percent of the costs of new product development. By 1983, it had more than 50 projects underway and 22 products already on the market, which in 1982 netted the corporation $3.3 million in royalties.

Numerous technical assistance programs are provided, especially to small businesses and entrepreneurial firms, including employee recruitment, skill training, facilities and business management, "how-to-start-your-own-business" market training, entrepreneurship training, and export promotion. Examples of these programs include the following:

- The **Indiana Institute for New Business Ventures** is a nonprofit state corporation to provide training and technical expertise to entrepreneurs exploring new investment opportunities. By 1985, it had considered 900 participants from 64 Indiana counties, spawning some local counterparts such as Ventures Fort Wayne. It operates a Seed Capital Network which provides computer matching of new ventures with private investors.

- The **Arizona Innovation Consortium** was established in 1985 to promote actions supportive of entrepreneurs, new business, and innovation in existing business. It is comprised of several Arizona entrepreneurs, presidents of three banks, directors of two "Entrepreneurial Centers" at Arizona universities, academic deans, legislators, representatives of the venture capital industry, and the state's director of economic development. Its focus is on disseminating information, supporting programs helpful to entrepreneurs, promoting public awareness, and building support on issues affecting entrepreneurs.

- **North Dakota** has created centers for innovation and business development at the University of North Dakota to provide technical assistance to businesses attempting to bring products to market. Services provided include assistance with patent applications, engineering and product testing, and business development and marketing plans.

- The **Delaware Small Business Development Center** was created in 1982 with a grant from the federal Small Business Administration. It assists existing small businesses and encourages the formation and growth of new business. In addition to the center's own professional staff, faculty from the University of Delaware and the Delaware Law School, as well as outside private consultants, are drawn upon to assist small businesses in start-up planning, feasibility assessment, loan applications, and economic, market, and financial research and analysis.

In our view, such efforts can best be viewed as experimental programs, to be carefully monitored and evaluated.

Far more significant to the creation and operation of business enterprise is the wide-ranging regulation of business by state government (see "State Regulation Affecting Business," page 50). Much has been learned about regulation at the federal level that is also applicable to the state and local levels. Regulation is an important and legitimate tool of public policy, but is subject to abuse. Counterproductive state regulations, including barriers to innovation and competitive adjustment, result from many causes. They may be well-intended but ill-conceived and unrealistic, be promoted by businesses seeking to protect themselves from competition, or be unduly motivated by the wish to gain political advantage by playing upon voter concerns. Regulations that may have been justifiable at the time they were enacted can become obsolete and counterproductive as economic circumstances change.

The regulation of capital markets is of particular importance to economic vitality. There is little evidence to support the contention that there

STATE REGULATION AFFECTING BUSINESS

- **Banking.** Bank and thrift institution failures have focused attention on regulatory procedures. The trend toward interstate banking raises questions about the authority of states to affect the nation's financial system.

- **Health Care.** Some states have tightened regulations for Medicare and Medicaid programs. A few, most prominently Minnesota, have moved toward a competitive market model.

- **Agriculture.** States establish quality standards for agricultural products and monitor consumer and crop safety. One study found 1,500 restrictions in eleven western states on interstate trade in agricultural products.[a]

- **Housing.** States establish construction and housing codes and regulate the siting and operation of condominiums and cooperatives.

- **Energy.** Gas and electric companies are regulated by states.

- **Telecommunications.** States regulate telecommunications companies and authorize local governments to regulate cable television, although efforts are underway in some 27 states to promote regulatory reform and reduce regulation of telecommunications common carriers.

- **Securities.** The recent trend toward corporate mergers has heightened state interest in securities regulation.

- **Occupations.** States establish entry requirements for some 500 occupations. One study estimates that such restrictions increase the earnings of those occupations by 12 percent, and another maintains that they are used to block the entry of minorities.[b]

- **Prices.** States regulate or indirectly affect the prices of such key goods and services as gas, electricity, telephone, taxicabs, health care, mass transit, and water and sewer services.

- **Labor Relations and the Work Force.** State laws set the framework that governs labor-management relations.

- **Consumer Protection.** Consumer protection, product liability, and truth-in-lending laws are in effect in every state.

- **Environmental Protection.** States establish environmental standards that are frequently stricter than federal laws.

- **Risk, Liability, and Dispute Resolution.** These issues are affected by state contract and tort law and by laws governing antitrust, consumer protection, product liability, truth-in-lending, occupational health and safety, environmental protection, and civil rights.

a. Steven G. Craig and Joel W. Sailors, "A Destructive War Between the States," *Wall Street Journal*, January 1985.
b. Roger J. Vaughan, Robert Pollard, and Barbara Dyer, *The Wealth of States*, pp. 52-56, citing Craig and Sailors, "A Destructive War Between the States," and Walter Williams, *The State Against Blacks*, (McGraw Hill Paperbacks, 1982).

are major "gaps" in capital markets, although it is likely that capital markets would operate more efficiently by permitting financial institutions to "price risk" more competitively.[6] The serious problems of the savings and loan industries in Ohio and Maryland provide evidence that elimination of all regulation is not necessarily practical. Regulation in capital markets, as in other areas of state responsibility, needs to be regularly reviewed in accordance with changing economic circumstances.

Awareness of international competitiveness and the potential of foreign markets have spawned interest in programs to promote exports. Florida and Georgia have established a joint information bank to identify institutions and people within those states with information on foreign markets and cultures. State foreign trade development programs include operational financing programs, foreign office representation, trade missions, trade shows, sales lead dissemination, how-to handbooks, newsletters, referrals to local export services, language banks, market studies, one-to-one counseling, seminars, and conferences.[7] Here, as in other enterprise development programs, we caution state officials to look for those instances where private initiative is not possible, and to proceed on an experimental basis with clearly established means for monitoring and evaluating new efforts. It is important that state activities in international markets be coordinated with the federal government to assure that states' efforts do not work against national interests.

QUALITY OF LIFE

The effect of a state's quality of life on economic development is elusive because it is the sum of so many factors (see Appendix B, Figure B-6). State government plays a major role in each of these factors.

Many states have found that business-location decisions are heavily influenced by quality-of-life considerations and therefore supplement their promotional materials with information about physical, recreational, cultural, and community amenities. A key element of the quality of life for businesses and their employees is an environment that encourages innovation, entrepreneurship, and risk taking. The Silicon Valley area of California has acquired a reputation for its vitality and innovative spirit, features that attract and help retain creative people and businesses. Alexander B. Trowbridge, President of the National Association of Manufacturers, attributes a large part of New England's economic resurgence to the region's "atti-

---

6. Roger J. Vaughan, Robert Pollard, and Barbara Dyer, *The Wealth of States*, p. 75.

7. National Conference on State Legislatures, *The States and International Trade: New Roles in Export Development (A Legislator's Guide)* (Denver, Colorado: 1985).

tudinal infrastructure that encourages imagination, innovation, and investments."[8]

Also important is the quality of public services. Minnesota recognizes the importance of a high quality-to-cost ratio in its public services as part of its economic strategy. To improve this ratio, the state's leaders have attempted to redesign public service systems by decentralizing responsibility for service delivery, permitting competition among providers, and allowing for choice by consumers.

FISCAL MANAGEMENT

As many as fifteen states reduced taxes in 1985 for the purpose of stimulating economic growth. A multiyear, multi-billion-dollar program in New York State to lower and restructure taxes and to reduce outstanding debt was undertaken in 1985 in the belief that "stable and predictable taxes are critical to business plans for economic expansion."[9]

Frequent or sudden changes in taxes, unfair tax burdens, or unnecessary and complicated record keeping can inhibit the ability of business to plan future investment and growth. Personal taxes that affect the ability to attract and retain high-salaried employees can be as important as business taxes in making location decisions.[10]

Inequitable and unproductive tax structures in a state can retard and distort growth by placing uneven tax burdens on different kinds of economic activity.[11] For example, taxation by a state on earnings from foreign activities of domestic businesses or the domestic subsidiaries of foreign firms through the use of the so-called unitary tax can be self-defeating for the state's economy. Such taxation by states is difficult to justify when economic development is a priority.*

It is equally important to assure that stable and evenhanded fiscal management provides adequate revenues for needed public services, and business leaders should make it clear that the private sector will support raising needed revenues.

---

8. University of Massachusetts in cooperation with the Northeast-Midwest Congressional Coalition, *New England's Role in Enhancing America's Competitiveness*, (Amherst: 1985), p. 15.

9. Roger J. Vaughan, *State Taxation and Economic Development* (Washington, D.C.: Council of State Planning Agencies, 1979).

10. The Governor's Council on Fiscal and Economic Priorities (New York State), *Changes in New York State Taxes to Spur Economic Development* (November 16, 1984).

11. Robert Kleine and John Shannon, "Characteristics of a Balanced and Moderate State-Local Revenue System," (paper presented before the National Conference of State Legislatures, Denver, Colorado, October 1985) pp. 15-17.

---

*See memorandum by JAMES Q. RIORDAN (page 89).

Federal tax reform has important implications for state tax structures and economic development policies. This is particularly true for the thirty states whose tax codes are coupled to the federal code, but it is important to all states since changes in the deductibility of state and local taxes, bond interest, or business expenses may result in important changes in the state and local fiscal equation.

THE UNSEEN EFFECTS OF A BUSINESS TAX

Washington State's business and occupation (B&O) tax is imposed on business gross income with no deductions for costs of doing business. Thus an integrated bakery that processes the flour, and bakes, packages, distributes, and retails bread, pays the B&O tax on the final retail product at a rate of .471 percent. The non-integrated baking retailer, by contrast, might pay the accumulated tax on each stage of the process — e.g., on the flour processer, the baker, the packager, and the distributor — which could total 1.5 percent, triple the tax paid by the integrated firm.

SOURCE: *Report of the CityClub Committee on Economic Development,* CityClub, Seattle, April 1986, p. 23.

Part II: Institutions

There is no simple formula by which the vast range of state government actions that affect economic performance can be neatly combined in an economic strategy. Conditions vary among states — developing fresh water supplies may be an urgent priority in one state while it is unnecessary in another. Times change — a state's priority to reduce unemployment necessarily shifts if a booming economy produces labor shortages. Knowledge and theory evolve — an exclusive focus on attracting industry from out of state makes little sense in light of abundant findings that business relocation from one state to another is small in comparison with business generation within a state economy.

Each state needs to tailor its own economic strategy to its particular conditions and to modify that strategy as changing conditions and new knowledge may warrant. Consequently, the institutional structure and process by which a strategy is developed and implemented is as important as a one-time prescription for economic strategy that can soon become outdated.

Common deficiencies in the institutional framework for economic affairs in most states include the following:

- *State economic policy is narrowly defined and tends to be equated with the state agency that bears the "economic development" label.* Even though there is widespread recognition of the broader reach of economic issues, state organizational structure continues to define economic concerns in terms of the traditional responsibilities of the department of economic development (or commerce) — recruitment, financial incentives to business, small-business assistance, and so on.

- *Efforts at broader definition usually fail to be translated into a cohesive strategy or implemented in a coordinated fashion.* Few states appear to have developed institutional mechanisms that effectively link key elements of economic strategy so that their implementation matches their conceptual connection.
- *Economic concerns are defined with an insufficient view to the long run.* Because the principal motivating force driving top state officials is the election cycle, it is rare that policy genuinely looks beyond the next gubernatorial or legislative election. Because private-sector groups, the media, and the public frequently lack understanding of the connection between current actions and long-term economic performance, there is little incentive for elected officials to make decisions for the long term.
- *In the absence of a broader and longer-term perspective, de facto economic policy at the state level is determined by numerous isolated decisions and driven by individual administrative and political agendas.* There is no reason to believe, and every reason to doubt, that the pursuit of so many conflicting agendas will produce a result that is beneficial to the state's economic health.

We believe that needed institutional changes require two principal ingredients: 1) *leadership,* **by which individuals improve the performance of the institutions for which they have responsibility; and 2)** *partnership,* **by which alliances are formed among groups that have common and/or complementary interests that are best pursued through joint action.** The final two chapters analyze each of these ingredients in turn.

Chapter 5

Leadership: Taking Personal Initiative

NORTH DAKOTA
OHIO
OKLAHOMA
OREGON
PENNSYLVANIA
RHODE ISLAND
SOUTH CAROLINA
SOUTH DAKOTA
TENNESSEE

Leadership is needed to intelligently diagnose economic forces, present a bold but practical vision of the state's economic future, and motivate people to act in pursuit of that vision.

Leadership requires political support, institutional authority, intellectual and moral credibility, and personal appeal. The governor is expected to possess most of these attributes and to be in the best position to assume leadership on issues that affect the state's economy. But initiative is essential as well from other leaders: legislators, other top government officials, business executives, labor leaders, university administrators and academicians, heads of nonprofit organizations, community and political leaders, and editors and journalists.

AN ECONOMIC LEADERSHIP CHECKLIST

There are eight steps that we urge these leaders to take.

1) **Recognize the importance of the state economy to other facets of life in the state.** Leaders in many spheres — education, the arts, social services, health, religion, politics, business — have goals that are legitimate and important in themselves. However, all these institutions benefit from a strong economy, and all suffer when economic weakness increases the competition for limited resources. In turn, each of these spheres can contribute to a strong economy.

2) **Become educated about the nature of economic change in the world and its effect on the state.** Leaders in some states have taken this responsibility seriously. For example, government, business, and university officials in Massachusetts have begun working with the Harvard Business School to assess the vulnerability of Massachusetts's high-technology

industry to foreign competition and to consider whether Massachusetts can learn from the Japanese approach to economic strategy. Leaders in other states should consider not only the potential for increasing their knowledge but also the advantage to be achieved by doing so.

3) **Identify and join with other leaders who share an interest in promoting the state's economy.** The multiplicity of groups and the diffusion of power make it difficult for any one leader to mobilize sufficient energy and support for complex and long-term undertakings. Leaders can, however, work with other leaders who have shared interests. (For a detailed discussion of these partnership opportunities, see Chapter 6.)

4) **Insist on sound diagnosis as a foundation for state economic strategy.** Most states have the analytical and theoretical expertise and practical experience to analyze the economy, critically assess theoretical propositions, and weigh the merits of new approaches. The problem, more often than not, is how to assemble that diagnostic capability and put it to use.

There is no monopoly on economic wisdom, and there should be no institutional monopoly on economic intelligence within a state. (See Chapter 2 for a discussion of ways to diagnose the state economy.)

5) **Participate in shaping a vision of the state's economic future.** The reach of economic concerns is so broad that no single source is likely to have all the information, knowledge, and insight needed to assure that state economic strategy is grounded in reality and adjusted according to changing circumstances. Participation by a broad spectrum of leaders is important to ensure that the vision addresses the long-term economic health of the state as a whole and is not biased by the short-term pressures of elections, narrow political agendas, or the performance of individual businesses.

6) **Identify completable actions compatible with the state vision, and join with other leaders to create the environment that will motivate people to undertake and complete these actions.** As we indicated in Chapter 4, the range of actions affecting the economy is vast. Careful selection is required to identify actions that are both completable and will have some effect. A key responsibility of leadership is to establish the link between long-term vision and short-term actions. There is no clear-cut, mechanical way of doing this; it requires the judgment and sustained involvement of responsible leaders.

7) **Determine the limits of the existing institutional framework for pursuing vital economic objectives and make adjustments as required.** If the agenda of completable projects would yield insignificant results, it may suggest that the structure or process by which economic strategy is determined and carried out is deficient. Institutional arrangements for economic strategy vary widely among the states. In general, however, common deficiencies reflect the failure to adjust conventional institutional arrangements to keep pace with changing conditions.

8) **Require that programs be monitored and periodically evaluated to assure public accountability and necessary adjustments.** Lack of monitoring is a weakness in many economic policies. (For a discussion of the reasons, see Chapter 2.) Because of their experimental nature, it is to be expected that many new state economic programs will not live up to their promise. Leaders should acknowledge this, and they should insist that clearly unproductive programs be modified or terminated. State leaders should be vigilant in spotting unethical or illegal activities; practices such as a periodic external audit of government financial accounts should be routinely required.

THE GOVERNOR AND THE EXECUTIVE BRANCH

The governor's leadership responsibility and potential in economic matters derive from four of his or her principal roles. As the state's top elected official, the governor represents a statewide political constituency in setting economic priorities and determining trade-offs among competing goals. The governor is also chief executive of the state government and thus its top planner and manager. It is the governor who makes key decisions with respect to appointments, directives to administrative agencies, the submission of bills and budgets to the state legislature, and the issuance of regulations. As the representative of state government, the governor negotiates with business, labor, local government, and other institutions in the state that affect the economy. In dealings beyond the state's borders — with other states, the federal government, foreign governments, and national corporations — the governor is the emissary for the state.

Governors have been directly involved in the development of economic strategy in at least twenty-two states. But they are frequently frustrated in their efforts to get a grip on economic matters. This is partly due to the tendency to conceive of economic development as a *function*, like transportation, education, or health care, that can be assigned to a single agency.[1] Most governors understand that the effect of state policy on the economy ranges far beyond the activities of the traditional state department of commerce or economic development. For example, the Nevada State Plan for Economic Diversification and Development specifically recognizes investments in education, infrastructure, and water supply as part of its economic development strategy. Nonetheless, the term "economic development" continues to define a narrow range of programs that focus on attracting and expanding business. These programs are important, but they should be viewed more strictly as "enterprise development" that is only one

---

1. National Governors' Association, *Revitalizing State Economies*, p. 10.

part of a broader economic strategy. (See Appendix C: The Evolution of Economic Development Agencies.)

The governor can take the first step toward a unifying strategy by articulating a concept of economic development that recognizes the broad range of forces and agencies that affect it. The limits of political practicality and government resources require that the governor focus on a few important, high-leverage themes. But the selection of those themes should be based on a broad consideration of economic issues and should not be dictated by the conventional formulation of more narrowly defined economic programs.

A successful economic program requires the governor's attention to five key executive functions: economic intelligence, policy development, oversight of agency activities, development of coalitions and partnerships, and media relations. These functions can be arranged in a host of different ways, depending on the management styles, personalities, abilities, and political-governmental culture in each state.

We recommend that governors acquire economic expertise within the executive office of the governor as part of an office of planning, an office of policy development, or as a separate office of economic affairs or council of economic advisors. Wherever located, economic analysis should be closely associated with general planning or policy development in recognition of its connection with numerous state programs and its importance to the state as a whole.

Governors have attempted to bring coherence to economic policy in a variety of ways. Some simply rely on key personal aides, charging one or two top staff people with the responsibility of identifying priorities for economic improvement. Others establish semi-formal core groups for economic policy, that may be made up of personal staff, heads of the planning, policy development, management and budget, public relations offices, and some key agencies.

In nineteen states, governors have established formal cabinet councils made up of cabinet heads whose departments are involved with some aspect of economic policy. The extensive membership of most such economic councils — including representatives from the departments of economic development, transportation, education, finance, licensing, employment, natural resources, agriculture, and possibly health and human services — is an indication of the breadth of economic concerns. Economic cabinet councils essentially replicate the state cabinet under a different name and are likely to be perfunctory if they do not command the direct personal attention of the governor. To be effective, cabinet councils for economic affairs should be chaired by the governor or the lieutenant governor, or by a knowledgeable cabinet officer who is a close associate of the governor. The council should be given a professional staff, and the staff director should be appointed by the chair or the governor.

To expand their access to economic knowledge and increase their ability to build coalitions for economic strategy, governors should also call upon capable people outside the public sector. Some state economic strategies have been developed by small groups of policy makers, academics, consultants, and citizen advisors. In Michigan, for example, the governor appointed an aide to head a task force consisting mainly of academicians to prepare a report, *The Path to Prosperity,* that set out a state economic strategy. Virtually every governor has established advisory groups or task forces to address economic issues. Some of these groups have been highly successful; others have simply created ill will, in part because the governor ignored them once they were established.

Communication regarding economic strategy is as important as the strategy itself. The frequency with which the governor indicates an interest in economic affairs and the medium chosen for referring to it (including speeches, press conferences, selection of meetings, and formal directives and program initiatives) are critical to establishing a general sense of the issue's importance. Public understanding of economic affairs can often be limited. The governor's selection of themes and the forcefulness with which he articulates them can do much to build understanding and support for critical economic issues.

The attitude of state officials is an important signal to business of the seriousness of the state's economic program. Business leaders take particular interest in the actions and words of the governor as reflections of the state's attitude toward business.[2]

THE LEGISLATURE

The legislature plays an important role in economic policy through the many largely unconnected actions it takes in its law making, budgetary, and oversight functions. The legislature also works out the complex aid distribution formulas that determine which parts of the state get what share of state grants.

Some state legislatures have taken the initiative in fashioning economic strategy, creating new institutions, amending laws and regulations, exercising their oversight powers in scrutinizing existing programs, or otherwise promoting new approaches to economic issues. The capability of some legislatures to deal with contemporary economic problems has been

---

2. Yankelovich, Skelly, and White, Inc., *The Business Climate in Wisconsin,* prepared for the Department of Development, State of Wisconsin, May 1984.

enhanced through the development of competent professional staff, improved legislative organization, and the election of knowledgeable legislators.

In 1982, the California legislature attempted to improve its organization for dealing with economic affairs by creating a Committee on Economic Development and New Technologies with subcommittees on international trade and investment, rural economic development, and biotechnology. A Committee on Small Business was also created to determine ways to stimulate new enterprise. The California State Senate, in 1984, established the Select Committee on Long-Range Policy Planning to examine the state's industrial competitiveness and recommend policies to promote economic progress through the year 2000.

However, few legislatures have played a leadership role in economic policy. Most are reactive, both to executive initiatives and to events in general, and are politically ill-disposed and poorly organized to undertake comprehensive or long-range analysis and planning. The time horizon of any elected official is determined by election cycles, and legislators' agendas tend naturally to focus on the concerns of their districts, the issues of the moment before the committees on which they serve, and the particular interests of their supporters. Few legislatures exercise systematic oversight of administrative agencies, and regular program evaluation is rare.

Most legislatures have at least one committee with jurisdiction over economic affairs. Its duties usually correspond to the industrial recruitment and business expansion activities of the department of economic development. Numerous other committees concern themselves with topics of economic importance, such as transportation, education, natural resources, labor, taxation, and regulation.

One of the most important economic policy roles of the legislature is to screen the thousands of bills introduced during each legislative session and reject the numerous proposals that would be harmful to the state economy. For example, more than 8,000 bills are introduced into the Massachusetts legislature each year. Given the volume of legislation, the clerk of the state senate plays a significant role in determining whether bills survive to be considered and whether economic bills are assigned in a way that facilitates or impedes comprehensive consideration.

Most legislatures require that a fiscal note or fiscal-impact statement accompany a bill estimating its cost to the state government. Legislatures should also consider a more systematic assessment of the costs and benefits to the state economy of major legislative proposals.

State legislatures could strengthen their economic policy role to some extent by changing the way they are organized to deal with economic matters. **Each house of the legislature should establish a mechanism for linking**

legislative proposals and committee activities that have major impact on the state economy. Similarly, the two houses of the legislature should create a joint mechanism to coordinate the economically related activities of the legislatures. Such mechanisms might take the form of standing committees, ad hoc committees on economic affairs, leadership conferences, staff committees, or conferences. The important thing is to reconcile the differences in approaches to economic affairs in each house and to provide the legislature with a mechanism for considering economic issues in a more coherent manner.

State legislatures should develop their own independent economic expertise. Economic analysts working in policy development, research, audit, or fiscal analysis units can provide objective assessment of the economic impact of legislative actions. Some legislatures have already established such units.

BUSINESS

Until recently, businesses not directly regulated by the state have often shown little interest in state government. But during the past decade, and particularly in the 1980s, a growing number of business executives have come to appreciate the impact of state government on business. Some businesses have found it prudent to take an interest in the process by which a state responds to plant closings, large-scale layoffs, and other signs of a poorly performing economy.

Some are also realizing the importance to the state of a stable and effective long-range economic strategy. Private-sector representatives have played an active role recently in developing economic strategies in twenty-eight states and are reported to have been totally inactive in only five states.[3]

In today's business environment, however, it may be difficult for executives to justify time given to community activities or long-term projects. Competition is fierce, profit margins in many industries are low, takeovers are a threat, and the economic environment is volatile. Chief executive officers are sensitive to potential criticism from members of their boards or from stockholders regarding time spent on activities not directly relevant to the company's interests. Some business executives are not aware of the productive public-private partnerships that have flourished at the local level in recent years, or of their applicability at the state level.

We view these developments with concern. It has never been a simple

---

3. National Governors' Association, *Revitalizing State Economies*, p. 10.

matter to establish a direct link between the bottom-line interests of a business and the long-term health of the state economy in order to justify a CEO's time and contribution to broad economic concerns. The time that the head of a firm, large or small, can spend on long-term economic or community improvement is, of course, limited. After all, there is no long term for a company that fails. Yet, lack of support for the improvements essential to regional economic health can jeopardize the company's chances for success. **Private-sector leaders should recognize the impact of state government action on their businesses, and they should take the time to address issues of state policy that can affect the business climate for their firms.**

Business, of course, includes a wide variety of enterprises. The problems faced by large corporations are different from those of established small businesses, and the needs of growing firms are different from those of stable or declining firms.

The diversity of business views is reflected in the multiplicity of organizations that represent them. Industry trade associations in every state are interested in legislation and regulations that have an impact on their industries. Traditional, broad-based business organizations, such as state chambers of commerce and state-level affiliates of the National Association of Manufacturers, are concerned with the impact of state policies on their members' operations.

Organizations also represent special enterprise sectors within states. For example, the Resource Development Council of Alaska focuses its attention on the natural resources that form the base of the Alaskan economy — oil, timber, minerals, coal, and fish.

The growing number and diversity of business organizations at the state level is well illustrated by Massachusetts. Until the mid-1970s, the Associated Industries of Massachusetts was the most vocal representative of business interests in the state. In 1977, the Massachusetts High Technology Council was formed by large high-tech companies. This was followed, in 1979, by the Massachusetts Business Roundtable, comprised of CEOs from the state's sixty largest employers. The 1980s have produced EMERGE, which represents small high-technology firms: the Massachusetts Software Council, a spin-off of software firms from the High Technology Council; the International Coordinating Council, composed principally of export-oriented firms; the Defense Technology Council; and the Massachusetts Biotechnology Council, which was established in 1986. The Small Business Association of New England, with over 2000 members, has been active since the 1930s. Since the 1970s, Jobs for Massachusetts has provided an informal forum for top government, business, and labor leaders.

In recent years, a number of CEO associations have been formed at the state level to address broader and long-term economic issues. For example:

- The *California Roundtable* in recent years has aroused broad business and civic concern over the faltering primary and secondary public education system in California. Objective research and the mobilization of business and public support have been instrumental in getting action to improve the school system.

- The *Business Roundtable of Pennsylvania* is a nonprofit, nonpartisan association of executives from major Pennsylvania corporations. It was organized in 1979 to promote economic growth and development, private-sector employment, and fiscal responsibility. The Roundtable seeks the direct participation of its members in the development of public policy, working in partnership with the legislative and executive branches of government. It has developed a long-term economic strategy for the state designed to navigate the transition from traditional to future economic activity.

- The *Washington Roundtable* was created to apply the knowledge, creativity, and leadership resources of its business members and their organizations to the most serious challenges facing the state. It conducts research and recommends action to improve the state's social and economic development. In its first three years, the Roundtable has generated two studies on K-12 and higher education, plus reports on estimated environmental spending, public works and capital needs, and the state's unfunded pension liability.

Similar groups are active in Minnesota, West Virginia, Massachusetts, Florida (the Group of 100), Hawaii, and several other states.

States also have a rich assortment of nonpartisan, public policy research organizations supported by business. Some, like the Pennsylvania Economy League, the California Taxpayers' Association, and the Texas Research League, have been active for many years. Many other organizations are being created in response to new economic pressures and the state's changing role. State tax reform organizations, many born of the tax revolt of the 1970s, have maintained a vitality and interest in state tax and fiscal policy and have expanded their agendas to include other issues affecting economic development. In Massachusetts, for example, Citizens for Limited Taxation was actively involved in the state referendum on Proposition $2^1/_2$ in 1979 and remains involved in state tax and fiscal policy as it affects economic development.

There are countless projects sponsored by individual industries or companies working with federal, state, and local governments. Numerous nonprofit organizations influence the state economy and have become involved in state policy formulation.

This diversity of business groups is a reflection of economic dynamism and vitality and the heterogeneity of the private sector in many states. The varying objectives and philosophies of different organizations add a richness of perspective and energy that can strengthen state economic strategy.

However, this diversity can also produce a fragmented and even contradictory vision for the state economy. **Just as state governments need to be certain that each of their important functions is contributing to long-term economic strength, business associations need to consider whether their organizational objectives are serving not just the interests of individual firms or industries, but the overall performance of the state economy as well.**

This can be accomplished in different ways. Private-sector leaders in some states may choose to create umbrella associations broad enough to encompass the diversity of views among state businesses. In other states, private sector leaders may feel that they do not need a formal organization to join forces on issues they all believe are important to the state's long-term economic health. In some states, business leaders may simply compete to have their individual views prevail in establishing state economic policy. The route chosen depends on the nature of the state economy, as well as on the interests and personal styles of business leaders. **The important thing is that the business leadership in each state should recognize the critical contribution the private sector can make to the long-term health of the state economy by identifying and supporting policies that move beyond the narrow interests of individual firms and industries.**

LOCAL GOVERNMENT

Local governments began to become extremely active in economic affairs in the early 1970s, for many of the same reasons that later motivated the states. Many of the larger local governments have established aggressive, entrepreneurial, and sophisticated programs to improve their economies, and these programs may rival or surpass those of their states. Local programs typically include a department of economic development and/or one or a series of economic development corporations. Mayors and county executives are frequently active in promoting the local economy through special programs, improved management of government programs affecting the economy, contacts with the local business community, promotional trips throughout the United States and abroad, and active representation of the local jurisdiction in negotiations with neighboring local governments and state and federal agencies. In Wisconsin, for example, 265 local governments have economic development programs.[4]

The approach to state economic strategy presented in this statement is, in general, also applicable to the larger local governments. One exception to this is that a local government's attention is more sharply focused on the details of a smaller economic region. Another is that local governments do not have the basic legal powers enjoyed by state government, except insofar as they are granted those powers by the state. **It is important that local governments be viewed as key participants in the development and execution of state economic strategy.**

MEDIA

Newspapers, magazines, and television and radio stations are not simply observers and reporters of events, economic or otherwise. What journalists choose to write and editors choose to release directly affects what the public believes and, therefore, what state officials decide to do. For example, state leaders have learned that they can get media attention by attracting large new businesses to the state. The media, in turn, give prominent coverage to such events, partly because state leaders use these events as standards by which to judge their performance. The race by different jurisdictions to win the prize of a major new facility, such as the General Motors Saturn plant, has drama, specific objectives, and clear winners and losers.

The media can help to improve state economic policy by assessing the real economic benefit of attracting major facilities, especially in comparison with the costs associated with elaborate financial packages, and by giving greater attention to the more complex and longer-term process by which jobs are created and sustained. Some journalists provide a genuine public service in challenging counterproductive policies while covering the more significant developments in state economic activity. Journalists and editors need to take account of the vast changes that have occurred in world competitiveness and in the role of the states in order to provide their audience with a more accurate picture of both the problems and the potentials of state economic strategies.

---

4. *State Policy Reports,* Vol. 3, Issue 16 (August, 1985), p. 11.

OTHER IMPORTANT INSTITUTIONS

Other important state institutions also have influential economic roles.

LABOR

Labor can have a significant impact on the business climate in the state. Statewide labor organizations are politically powerful in many states and can influence legislation that affects the workplace, costs, and the state's image. Labor is also knowledgeable about particular economic conditions and can help to fashion a state's economic strategy. In some states, labor is represented in statewide economic strategy groups, such as the Resource Development Council in Alaska, the Economic Alliance in Michigan, and Minnesota Wellspring.

UNIVERSITIES

Universities help educate the work force, attract talented people and enterprises, conduct basic research, and help apply research to commercial products. Universities themselves constitute an enterprise of major importance to regional and local economies. University officials, both administrators and academicians, can play major leadership roles as community leaders and as sources of knowledge about the state economy.

FOUNDATIONS

Foundations are in an especially advantageous position to promote a broader and longer-term perspective on state economics by supporting objective research and diagnosis of state and local economic conditions and encouraging experimentation with promising new approaches to economic development.

NOT-FOR-PROFIT ORGANIZATIONS

Not-for-profit organizations constitute a significant part of state economies. Health, education, and research institutions, in particular, may represent not only a sizable component of a state's economy but also an important generator of economic growth. Many of the amenities associated with the quality of life are provided by nonprofit institutions.

PUBLIC AUTHORITIES

Public authorities in many states are responsible for vital functions that profoundly influence the economy. Investment decisions on port facilities, rail service, airport service, utilities, and water supply directly influence the state economy and impact the pattern of private investment.

Leaders in all of these and other important institutions can play a key role in improving state economies.

Chapter 6
Partnership: Linking Common Interests

Individuals working within their own institutions can only accomplish so much. Joint efforts and new institutional arrangements are required to bridge the many gaps among groups with common goals and mutually dependent capabilities.

Many important alliances will not be easy to forge, involving as they do traditional adversaries who will continue to view their individual interests as being in conflict with those of other groups. But conditions that gave rise to these rivalries and antagonisms may have changed enough to open up new opportunities for partnership. Competitive threats from outside the state can foster a sense of mutual interest. During the 1960s and 1970s, adversarial groups in cities learned that they had a common interest in economic survival. Now there are signs in many states that mutual interest in the state economy is assuming relatively greater importance in shaping political conduct.

Partnerships of several types are needed: within state government; between the public and private sectors; among government, industry, and universities; between the federal government and the state; between state and local governments; among states; and in civic organizations.

PARTNERSHIP WITHIN STATE GOVERNMENT

Partnership within state government should begin within the executive and legislative branches. We addressed the means of coordinating economic policy in both branches in Chapter 5, but it bears repeating that internal cohesiveness is essential if broader alliances are to be effective.

In many states, political antagonism between the governor and the legislature or between political parties is a major stumbling block to the development of a coherent economic strategy. Private-sector leaders in several states have approached the governor or legislative leaders with suggestions for economic improvement only to be told that working with the other branch of government is either politically impossible or undesirable.

Healthy tension between the executive and legislative branches of government is to be expected. Unfortunately, political dissension too often is rooted solely in narrow concerns of personal and factional power. Because economic issues are complex, and because the results of important actions materialize only in the long run, the opportunities for posturing and narrow political maneuvering are all too great.

Checking such inclinations is not easy. Admonition for antagonists to get along with each other is not likely to be persuasive in the face of powerful political forces that work in opposite directions. What can be helpful, short of direct political action, is changing the terms of the debate. Defining economic issues in their broader context can help demonstrate the link between short-term actions and their long-term effects on state residents. A shared vision that is strong enough to override narrow interests can contribute to this purpose.

Cooperative efforts are possible despite natural political rivalry. Indiana's development of a strategic plan enjoyed bipartisan support in large measure because of the leadership and cooperation of the state's top Republican and Democratic politicians. Republican Governor Robert Orr and Lieutenant Governor John Mutz, who is also ex-officio head of the state's Department of Commerce, were intent on creating an active economic development program. John Hillenbrand, president of the Indiana Chamber of Commerce and also the Democratic nominee for governor (he was defeated by Orr), initiated the idea for a state strategic plan for economic development.

PUBLIC-PRIVATE PARTNERSHIP

Effective collaboration between government and business is impeded by a lack of appreciation on both sides of the forces with which the other must contend. Business executives seek well defined objectives and schedules that give precision to their efforts. They are accustomed to narrowing goals to achievable targets and responding to pressures that require demonstrable accomplishment in meeting those targets. In contrast, elected officials tend to avoid sharply defined choices and precise objectives against which their performance will be judged. They face numerous constituencies with conflicting interests. Consequently, they often attempt to synthesize, blur, or postpone issues that will alienate politically powerful groups. At the other extreme, they may attempt to divide and define issues so sharply for political advantage that a potential synthesis or compromise of interests becomes impossible.

Such inclinations on both sides, however understandable, can create impediments if carried to extremes. Excessive concern with specific targets can alienate important political constituencies and may ignore broader public concerns. The avoidance of painful political decisions or attempts to please all sides can result in delay or costly action. Exaggerated differences can stiffen antagonisms and undermine debate and compromise.

Understanding these inclinations, business and government leaders, especially those responsible leaders who must contend with the more extreme forms of behavior among their colleagues, can help each other in addressing difficult policy issues. Each brings to the task a background that can help curb the excessive tendencies in the other. The economic issues facing states involve legitimate and complex political questions of risk, equity, health and safety, environmental impact, and public trust that cannot always be simply resolved. By the same token, the state's economic future is endangered when the legitimate need to deal with complex and conflicting values deteriorates into a directionless attempt simply to appease every political interest or reinforce political loyalties.

At least fifteen states have attempted to bridge the gap by establishing committees or task forces with public and private representation to recommend an economic strategy.

- Washington's Committee on High Technology Training and Advancement was established in 1982 to examine state technical education, training, and assistance programs; to identify barriers to high-technology development and growth; and to promote high-technology training and advancement. Like its counterparts in other states, this thirty-member committee was structured to represent a broad range of interests: government (four members), the state legislature (four), education and technical training (eight), business and high-technology industry (twelve), and labor (two).

California's experience with advisory boards during the administrations of two governors is instructive.

- In 1981, Governor Jerry Brown appointed the California Commission on Industrial Innovation, comprised of a high-level group of leaders from industry, labor, and education, including David Packard, chairman of Hewlett-Packard, and Steven Jobs, chairman of Apple Computer. Some of its recommendations were enacted, such as the university-business research joint venture, Microelectronics Innovation and Computer Research Operation at the University of California at Berkeley. However, much of the Commission's impact was lost when Brown left office in 1982.

- In 1983, Governor George Deukmejian established the Economic Advisory Task Force in response to concerns that California was suffering from a negative business image and growing competition from other states. It recommended a three-part strategy to "fix the product" (i.e., the state's business climate), "market the product" (through an aggressive promotional effort), and "support the sales force" (through state-local linkage and state agency coordination).[1] Recommendations of the task force are being implemented.

A few states have attempted to establish broadly-based institutions with public and private sector representation not just to develop but to participate in implementing a strategic plan.

- Indiana's strategic plan for economic development, *In Step with the Future...*, was produced with the involvement of representatives from industry, banking, labor, and the state universities. The Indiana effort produced not so much a written plan but a structure and process that would permit leaders to adapt to changing circumstances. The Indiana Economic Development Council was established to act as an internal guidance system that links state institutions as they relate to seven broad areas of economic concern: business climate, education and training, energy, infrastructure, technology, productivity, and finance and capital.

In some states, informal networks and patterns of communication have been especially constructive in linking the economic interests of the public and private sectors.

- In North Carolina, informal networks among leaders in government, business, and education played a major role in the development of the Research Triangle. "State leaders were sufficiently secure that they erected no curbs or other barriers holding back others who aspired to positions of state leadership, and their sense of responsibility for the state gave them broad social support. Just as North Carolina leaders, with no single large urban area, centered their philanthropy on the state, establishing the first state symphony in the 1930s and the first state art museum in the 1950s, so the modernizers thought of the state as a whole."[2]

- In Michigan, informal discussions among leaders in venture capital, education, and banking led to the establishment of several new institu-

---

1. Douglas Henton and Steven A. Waldhorn, "California: Inventing the Future," p. 69.

2. Ezra Vogel, *Comeback* (New York: Simon and Schuster, 1985), p. 243.

tions designed to strengthen the state's position in new manufacturing technology.

- In Massachusetts, informal interaction among leaders in government, education, and finance has been instrumental in building support for new economic initiatives. Periodic informal meetings among top government, business, and labor leaders have also served to address key issues regarding the state economy.

There is considerable experience with public-private partnership at the state level to deal with specific issues. CED's 1978 policy statement *Jobs for the Hard to Employ: New Directions for a Public-Private Partnership* strongly urged that the private sector be more actively involved in jobs programs. The subsequent creation of private industry councils and the strong state role under the Jobs Training Partnership Act of 1981 have provided a base for further partnership arrangements at the state level.

Many state governments have become more aggressive in putting together deals or arrangements with two or more participants to promote or facilitate specific projects. Most of these efforts are similar to efforts at the local level over the past decade. Participants might include a developer, business, university, neighborhood group, and municipal government, as well as the state government. The General Motors Training Program in Missouri, for example, combines efforts by the state government, the company, and the United Auto Workers to train workers in robotics for a new assembly plant in Weitzville, Missouri. Massachusett's pragmatic approach to arranging such deals has been viewed as a key to that state's economic strategy.[3]

In recent years, new public-private institutions chartered as public, nonprofit corporations have been created to deal with such economic concerns as venture capital, product development, technological research and development, and assistance to industry. These institutions draw on state experience with quasi-public industrial development authorities, which have been used since the 1930s to issue industrial development bonds and make guaranteed loans to business. At least thirty-two new organizations have been established in twenty-six states since 1983.[4]

- *Indiana's Corporation for Innovative Development* (CID) is a privately owned venture-capital investment company that makes equity-oriented direct investments in Indiana businesses. CID investors get a 30 percent tax credit, which generated $10 million. By 1985, it had invested $4 million to attract an additional $28 million from out-of-state investors.

---

3. David S. Broder, " 'New Deal-Making' Politics: Massachusetts Governor Develops a Machine," *The Washington Post*, February 10, 1986.

---

4. National Governors' Association, *Revitalizing State Economies*, p.10.

- *California Economic Development Corporation* is a new private, not-for-profit corporation that advises the governor on ways to improve cooperation between the state's public and private sectors. Its funding is from private donors, but its members are appointed by the governor.

GOVERNMENT-INDUSTRY-UNIVERSITY PARTNERSHIP

Businesses and universities are finding common ground for partnership. Many firms are seeking a stronger position in basic research and emphasizing continuing education for their professional staffs. Universities, in turn, are moving into interdisciplinary research that cuts across traditional academic departments, and many are seeking commercial application of their research and professional opportunities for their faculty. State governments have attempted to encourage that collaboration, and, as sponsors of public university systems, are directly involved in many new university-business partnerships.

Figure 2, pages 74 and 75, matches the needs of university and industry against each other to highlight both mutual interests and potential conflicts. (In some instances, a need is repeated in order to emphasize a correlation with more than one corresponding need from the other side.)

As the chart indicates, despite the publicity that is given to barriers to university-industry cooperation, there is a wide commonality of interests. One of the most powerful incentives for cooperation is that the cost of research (i.e., professionals, technicians, educators, and equipment) has skyrocketed. Sharing resources can help cut costs. The chart also reveals clear and recognized conflicts between academia and industry: academic freedom versus market-driven research, publishing research results versus confidentiality, ownership of patents versus control over research results, and best effort versus commitment to what is deliverable. Some of these conflicts derive from problems *within* universities, especially those concerning the role of academicians in commercially oriented research and development.

The proliferation of university-industry relationships defies simple categorization. The hundreds of arrangements made over the past several years are tailored to particular circumstances. They range from general support for basic research to focused application of marketable products. Virtually every area of practical science and technology has received attention, but the bulk of the activities and financing are in the life sciences, computers and microelectronics, and materials.

Institutional arrangements range from one-to-one agreements between a university and a firm to multiple-university/multiple-firm agreements and new organizations. In each case, the arrangement seeks to blend the variable goals of the institutions involved: in the case of industry, from gaining a window on science to developing marketable products; in the case of the universities, from a general interest in strengthening its research capability to the development of marketable products to finance university activities. Preliminary evaluation of these new institutional arrangements shows that there is no preferred formula for accomplishing these goals. Each state needs to develop arrangements compatible with its strategies, universities, and business community.

FIGURE 2

What Does Business Expect from Universities?
What Do Universities Expect from Business?

Research and Technology Transfer

University Needs	Business Needs
Real-life problems for research topics Freedom to pursue own research topics	Research that is relevant to business problems
Exciting research topics to attract leading faculty and students	Commitment to interdisciplinary research
Freedom to publish research results	Confidentiality of useful research results
Ownership of patents produced by research	Effective control over commercial application
Funding for research Funding for equipment and its maintenance	Leveraging of research and development outlays
Monetary and morale benefits associated with industry consulting and other liaison-type programs	Prestige from association with the university Access to professors Problem solving/troubleshooting Keeping up with developments in field Extension service benefits
Help in gaining access to government-funded projects	Leveraging of research and development outlays
Development of political allies outside the university	Access to technology Access to university facilities
Best-effort standard for directed research	Commitment to deliverables

There are five principal ways in which states are involved in university business partnerships: state-established centers, state grants to research centers, research incubators, small-business development centers, and research parks.

STATE-ESTABLISHED CENTERS

States have taken the initiative to establish new institutions for research and development.

- *Microelectronics Center of North Carolina (MCNC).* MCNC is a private, nonprofit corporation established in 1980 to develop a research and manufacturing capability in microelectronics. Its interest is to inte-

Curriculum and Teaching

University Needs	Business Needs
Curriculum that follows from research Funding for such research	Instruction that is relevant to industry needs
Developing contacts with potential employers	Access to bright students
Ability to offer exciting academic (e.g., co-op) programs	
Real-life problems for instruction and student research	Proper handling of proprietary data
Support for new curriculum developments	Interdisciplinary approach to scientific and technical teaching
	University promotion-tenure-compensation system that rewards more industry interactions

SOURCE: George D. Krumbhaar, Jr., "The Industry-University Connection and State Strategies for Economic Growth," unpublished prepared for CED, June 1985.

grate basic and applied research with commercial development by industry, focusing on the development and manufacture of the next generation of micron and submicron geometrically integrated circuits. Its governing board includes the state budget director, four citizens, two members appointed by the governor, and the presidents of the Research Triangle Institute and the five universities that are MCNC members. Biennial state budget appropriations now total $82 million; and private sources, principally thirty-three participating private firms, have contributed $12 million.

STATE GRANTS TO RESEARCH CENTERS

Business support for university research is widespread throughout the nation and has grown dramatically in the past ten years. State governments have also become increasingly involved in funding targeted research initiatives at specific universities.

- *New York Science and Technology Foundation* has over twenty years of experience in the promotion of statewide scientific and technological education as well as basic and applied research and development. It operates with a budget of $20 million and serves as a conduit between the private sector and academic communities to promote cooperative research and development ventures.

- *Arizona State University's Center for Excellence in Engineering* was developed when the Arizona legislature provided matching funds for specific research in engineering: solid-state electronics, design/manufacturing, thermosciences, energy systems, and transportation.

- *Ben Franklin Partnership.* The Ben Franklin Partnership is really six programs initiated by the state of Pennsylvania as part of a statewide economic strategy described in *Choices for Pennsylvanians.*[5]

RESEARCH INCUBATORS

Research incubators are facilities that provide a supportive environment for developing new products and services. They attempt to use the resources and environment of a university for business innovation.

- *Georgia's Advanced Technology Development Center,* created in 1980 on the campus of the Georgia Institute of Technology in Atlanta, acts as an incubator to assist small technology-based companies in a number of ways: helping to identify product markets; providing low-cost space; furnishing management, financial planning, and marketing assistance; and evaluating new products and ideas.

---

5. Commonwealth of Pennsylvania, Pennsylvania State Planning Board, *Choices for Pennsylvanians,* 1980.

- *Pennsylvania's Ben Franklin Challenge Grant Programs* established four new Advanced Technology Centers that oversee the development of incubators in close affiliation with universities throughout the state.

SMALL-BUSINESS DEVELOPMENT CENTERS

Many state programs to assist small businesses are directly linked to colleges and universities.

- *Delaware Small Business Development Center* draws on faculty from the University of Delaware and the Delaware Law School, who, aided by the Center's own staff, assist small businesses in start-up, planning, feasibility studies, loan applications, and other research.

- *Rhode Island Small Business Development Center* has a program similar to Delaware's. The center has been established at Bryant College.

RESEARCH PARKS

Research parks often provide facilities for small business development.

- The *University of Utah Research Park* is adjacent to the campus in Salt Lake City. A number of private companies in the park are spin-offs from the university itself.

In addition to these principal forms of involvement, states have been active in numerous but less intense ways (see Figure 3, page 78). Much of the success of these efforts will depend on how effectively each state can create a climate in which mutual gain can be recognized and pursued.

FEDERAL-STATE PARTNERSHIP

Changes in the world economy have been creating new economic responsibilities for the federal government, just as other economic responsibilities are being assumed by state and local governments. The principal macroeconomic tools — fiscal, monetary, exchange rate, and trade policy — will continue to reside with the federal government and are all the more important in an increasingly global economy.

At the same time, federal programs that have been mainstays of state economic development efforts are being sharply curtailed. President Reagan's fiscal 1987 budget recommended elimination of several development programs used by state and local government, including the Economic Development Administration (EDA), Urban Development Action Grants (UDAGs), the loan and loan-guarantee programs of the Small Business Administration (SBA), the community development loan program of the Farmer's Home Administration, and reduced funding for the Community Development Block Grants (CDBGs). State use of federal trade pro-

FIGURE 3

Less Intense Forms of State Government Involvement in University-Business Partnerships

Type of Linkage	Example	State Involvement
Long-term research agreements	Center for Biotechnology State University of New York (SUNY), at Stonybrook	Medium
Nonprofit corporation	Hawaii Institute for Electronics Research	Medium
Industrial cooperatives	Council for Chemical Research	Medium
Venture-capital programs	Institute for Ventures in New Technology (Texas A&M)	Medium
Multiuniversity grants aimed at specific academic problem	IBM cash and equipment grant (manufacturing and engineering)	Low
Cooperative research (National Science Foundation program)	Center for Polymer Research (Massachusetts Institute of Technology)	Low
Industrial affiliates	Robotics Institute (Carnegie-Mellon University)	Low
University-affiliated foundations	Wisconsin Alumni Research Foundation	Low
Entrepreneurship training	Center for Entrepreneurship Training at Carnegie-Mellon	Low
Large partnership contracts	Monsanto and Washington University	Low
One-on-one contracts, faculty consulting	Most engineering departments	Low
Shared equipment and/or facilities	Grumman Corporation/ State University of New York, Stonybrook	Low
Co-op student programs	Massachusetts Institute of Technology	Low
Service on university advisory boards	Arizona State University	Low
Group fund raising by industry for higher education	Massachusetts High Technology Council	Low

NOTE: The principal forms of state involvement, including state-established centers, grants to research centers, research incubators, small-business development centers, and research parks, are not shown on the chart but are described in the text.

grams, such as those provided by the Department of Commerce's International Trade Administration, has increased. We support efforts to lessen states' reliance on such federal programs, especially in light of efforts to reduce the federal deficit. At the same time, greater attention should be directed to determining how a reduced federal role in such programs can be most effective in supporting state economic development.

One of the most important federal policies affecting state and local development activities is the tax-exempt status accorded to municipal bonds. Tax-exempt, public purpose bond issues by state and local governments finance public works which can be critical to economic performance. There is far less justification, however, for private purpose, tax-exempt bonds issued by state and local authorities. Private purpose bonds soared as a proportion of all state-local bonds from 20 percent in 1975 to over 50 percent by 1985. Moreover, the overall volume and growth (jumping from $30 billion in 1975 to $85 billion in 1981) has drawn investable funds away from new plant and equipment and may have crowded out some private-sector investment. Small issue industrial revenue bonds, which expanded ten-fold between 1975 and 1981 to $13.7 billion per year, appear to have little impact on industrial location decisions and make little contribution to local employment growth. While there appears to be little gain from these bonds, they constitute a substantial drain on the federal treasury at a time when every effort should be made to reduce the deficit.

Steps were taken in the Tax Reform Act of 1982 to restrict the use of private purpose bonds. In Illinois, for example, industrial development bond issues had reached a level of $1 billion per year, but under the tighter restrictions were cut to about $250 million per year. Responding to these changes, the National Association of State Development Agencies recently created a nonprofit affiliate, American Development Finance, Inc., to help state development agencies make more productive use of the taxable bond market for development purposes.

We support the continued tax exemption for the interest on state and local government public purpose bonds, but urge substantial further restriction or elimination of the exemption for private purpose bonds, which distort capital markets and constitute an unjustifiable drain on the federal treasury.*

There are good reasons why it may make more sense for the states to attempt various approaches on a decentralized basis than for the federal government to undertake nationwide programs. Enterprise zones are a good example. Federal enterprise zone legislation, still pending in Congress, has been oriented toward tax and regulatory concessions. By 1985, twenty-seven states had adopted enterprise zone legislation and had designated a total of 170 zones. Another 430 enterprise zones have been established by local jurisdictions. States have shifted the orientation toward

---

*See memorandum by HENRY B. SCHACHT (page 89).

bringing government, business, and civic organizations together to revitalize communities through coordinated investment. Formal evaluation has yet to demonstrate that the benefits of enterprise zones exceed their costs, but it is reasonable to assume that the knowledge gained from the different approaches taken by the states will be useful in developing more effective approaches. If the zones prove not to be useful, or even counterproductive, individual states themselves will bear the consequences. Experience may also point to a more precise way in which the federal government could support the enterprise zone concept.

Shifting too much responsibility to the state level from either the federal or the local level could obscure the legitimate and important responsibilities these other levels of government have in promoting healthy economies. The financial collapse of many states in the 1830s after a period of robust experimentation and the violent passions stirred by the economic differences among the regions in the 1850s and 1860s are distant but instructive reminders.

Although state government in general has made impressive strides, differences in size, geography, demography, economic history, and political culture remain. Some states will do better in a more state-competitive environment; others will do less well, or perhaps their fortunes will decline. The implications of such differences for both national economic health and political harmony cannot be ignored.

The increased activity by state governments in international trade and investment should also be approached with caution. **States must refrain from actions that violate U.S. treaties and trade agreements with other countries, and, more generally, they must assure that their activities do not undermine United States foreign policy objectives.***

STATE-LOCAL PARTNERSHIP

Because states have broad constitutional powers to determine the structure, mission, legal authority, and financial capability of local governments, they have a special responsibility to conduct those responsibilities in a manner conducive to effective governmental and economic performance. Too often, local government powers are granted or limited by state action on the basis of prevailing political forces that have little concern for long-term economic impact on local communities and consequently on the state.

The economically critical function of education illustrates the problem. As states have assumed greater responsibility for the financing of pub-

---

*See memorandum by JAMES Q. RIORDAN (page 89).

lic schools,[6] they have also tended to take greater control of educational decision making. In CED's policy statement *Investing in Our Children: Business and the Public Schools* (1985), we strongly opposed this trend because we fear that tightening state control will jeopardize the bottom-up approach we believe essential to effective education (see "A 'Bottom-Up' Strategy for Education," below). To be sure, states should have an important role in setting educational standards, assuring adequate and fair school financing, and evaluating performance. But if they are to achieve their purpose of promoting effective education that will benefit the state economy, they must refrain from trying to run the schools themselves.

States have a major role to play in assuring that local governments have the legal, financial, and administrative capability and the political incentive to enhance the economic vitality of the sub-regions of the state, especially those in distress. Local governments in many metropolitan areas have managed to fashion government institutions that address common

---

6. Committee for Economic Development, *Investing in Our Children: Business and the Public Schools* (New York: 1985), p. 56.

A "BOTTOM-UP" STRATEGY FOR EDUCATION

Our recommendations form a "bottom-up" strategy that views the individual school as the place for meaningful improvements in quality and productivity. This strategy does not minimize the importance of states, localities, and the federal government in defining goals, setting priorities, and providing resources. Nor does it overlook the role that the state and local authorities must play when schools and school systems fail to meet minimum standards. The states should provide "top-down" guidance and support to local schools by establishing clear goals and high standards and by developing precise measuring tools to evaluate educational achievement. At the same time, the states should give the schools maximum freedom to develop and implement the methods that would best achieve those goals.

The focus of our recommendations, therefore, is on the individual school — its students, teachers, and administrators — and the community it serves. Our central concern is with the instructional process and the interaction between student and teacher. We give careful attention to the selection, training, motivation, compensation, and working conditions of the nation's present and future classroom teachers. We also place special emphasis on improving the management of the individual school, for we see many applicable lessons from business experience in handling professional employees and utilizing resources more effectively.

SOURCE: Committee for Economic Development, *Investing in Our Children: Business and the Public Schools* (New York, N.Y.: 1985), page 7.

metropolitan needs. For example, regional councils provide planning capability, and single-purpose agencies provide water, sewer, and transportation services. However, as metropolitan areas have expanded beyond suburban into exurban areas and beyond, and as new types of regional economies have taken shape, the challenge to local government has become almost insurmountable. Even in Nashville, which years ago consolidated its local government with that of surrounding Davidson County, the metropolitan area has expanded beyond the city-county boundary. The Boston metropolitan area, which spreads beyond the borders of Massachusetts, is now so extensive that it depends heavily on state government involvement in the provision of basic services. In Michigan, the industrial and financial center of Detroit, the research center of Ann Arbor, and the political center of Lansing constitute an economic region that only the state can encompass.[7]

In some metropolitan areas, the private sector has taken the initiative to forge stronger ties among both private and public organizations. For example, in 1982, the Long Range Planning Committee of the Greater Philadelphia Chamber of Commerce determined that a more effective structure was required to join groups in the five Pennsylvania counties of metropolitan Philadelphia to develop and implement a regional economic development strategy. The result is the Greater Philadelphia First Corporation (see "Private-Sector Regional Associations in the Philadelphia Metropolitan Area," page 83 opposite), which in 1985 released a strategic plan for the 1985-1990 period. It intends to expand this plan into a public-private strategic plan involving government, business, labor, and universities in the area's five Pennsylvania counties. It also hopes to establish closer working relationships with entities in the New Jersey portion of the Philadelphia metropolitan area.

Strategy 21, a similar approach in the Pittsburgh area, was used by the Allegheny Conference on Community Development, a long-standing private civic organization, to negotiate with state government. State leaders in Pennsylvania have discussed with local leaders the possibility of persuading the various regions of the state to prepare such partnership plans as building blocks for a state strategic plan.

Smaller cities, towns, and villages usually fall within the economic orbit of a larger metropolitan area. Rural areas, once almost exclusively agricultural, have taken on varied economic characters as agricultural, extractive, and urban economic activities have overlapped. Few of these areas possess municipal or county governments that encompass what could

---

7. Michael J. Piore and Charles F. Sabel in *The Second Industrial Divide* maintain that changes occurring in basic industrial organization increase the importance of "industrial districts" and requires a stronger role for regional and local institutions. (New York: Basic Books, Inc., 1984), p. 17.

be considered cohesive economic regions. In these cases, the state can link the components of such regions and thus has a special responsibility to address the economic problems that many of these areas face.

- Idaho has taken a regional approach to economic development within the state. By the establishment of "PRO-Idaho" (PRO stands for partnerships, resources, and opportunities), Idaho seeks to create partnerships between business, community, education, and government leaders for coordinating economic development activity. Six planning regions have been created and are represented on the Governor's Economic Development Advisory Council.

Many states have attempted to help local governments in their economic development efforts. Some states provide loans and loan-guarantee funding for special infrastructure projects and technical assistance to local governments for their development efforts. Two states have state-funded grant programs similar to the federal UDAG program.[8]

---

8. NGA, *Revitalizing State Economies*, p. 12.

PRIVATE-SECTOR REGIONAL ASSOCIATIONS IN THE PHILADELPHIA METROPOLITAN AREA

Five affiliated organizations have been created by the private sector, each with different but related tasks in furthering the development of the Metropolitan Philadelphia area. They are:

- *The Greater Philadelphia First Corporation* to consolidate and focus corporate leadership in economic development.

- *The Greater Philadelphia First Foundation* to provide a consolidated source for corporate funding of regional economic development projects and programs.

- *The Greater Philadelphia Chamber of Commerce* to serve as the principal regional business support organization and to speak on governmental affairs for the business community as a whole.

- *The Greater Philadelphia Economic Development Coalition* to serve as a regional public/private partnership developing strategies and priorities for future economic development.

- *The Urban Affairs Partnership* to serve as a partnership for urban affairs organizations to establish strategies and priorities on quality of life matters that directly or indirectly affect the region's future economic development.

SOURCE: *The Greater Philadelphia First Affiliates.*

Nonetheless, many local officials, although often in heated competition with one another, view state economic development policy as insensitive to local needs and even as an impediment to local efforts. A common complaint is that state promotional efforts are not in tune with local promotional efforts or otherwise play favorites with politically influential areas of the state. Local officials also complain that state programs outside the state economic development program (in such economically critical areas as highway construction, water and sewer systems, education, job training, employment security, financial regulation, and land-use management) do not support local economic development efforts. Officials in cities with high levels of unemployment are concerned that state efforts bypass central city problems and do not address the problems of the hard-to-employ.

We urge states to work more closely with city and county governments to create economic programs that reinforce one another. State-created offices of intergovernmental relations modeled after the federal Advisory Commission for Intergovernmental Relations exist in many states and can help to promote a broader view of state-local economic strategy and improve the coordination between state and local economic development programs. **We also urge private-sector leaders to work with their local governments to improve state-local partnerships.**

STATE-TO-STATE PARTNERSHIP

Every subnational economic region in the United States, including the New England, Middle Atlantic, Midwest, Southeast, West South Central, Southwest, Plains, Mountain, and Western regions, encompasses all or parts of several states. Interstate cooperation is required if the natural economic dynamics of such regions are not to be impeded and their mutual potential is to be realized. For example, some California leaders believe the state has more in common with Washington and Oregon in looking to exploit their location on the Pacific Rim than with Arizona, New Mexico, and the Southwest. A flow-of-funds study by the Federal Reserve Bank of New York determined that Buffalo may have more trade with Minneapolis than with New York City because of the Great Lakes connection.

We believe the creation of interstate regional institutions at the initiative of the states affords a major opportunity to deal with regional economic concerns. Such organizations as the Southern Growth Policies Board, the Coalition of Northeastern Governors, and the Western Governors Association address broader regional economic concerns.* Several regional organizations are establishing research and development institutions that will serve all the states in the region. Some have also developed joint marketing efforts in promoting the regional economy, especially in

---

*See memorandum by ELMER B. STAATS (page 90).

international markets. There is also growing interest in international partnerships, where states acting on their own or in concert with their neighbors work more closely with their counterparts abroad to enhance trade and investment linkages.

CIVIC PARTNERSHIP

In the end, the real test for states will be whether they have the ability to anticipate and adjust continually to the emerging economy. To do so will require elected officials who are knowledgeable and open to new ideas, leaders in all sectors who will participate constructively in testing new economic approaches, and a citizenry that is aware of the serious competitive challenge and supportive of attempts to confront it. Meeting the economic challenge will require, in short, civic partnership.

Civic institutions are important in raising issues, analyzing issues, building consensus, advocating implementation, monitoring progress, and evaluating results. They can be close enough to the issues and institutions of government to know them but not so close that they have a vested interest or are afraid to raise unpopular issues or report unpopular findings. Because they can endure beyond elections, they can follow issues through to implementation and later evaluate them.

Cities have a far richer tradition of civic organization than states do.[9] People tend to identify more closely with their home town than with their state. Minnesota is one of the few states to have a well-established network of statewide civic institutions (see "Civic Organization in Minnesota," page 86). This is due in large part to the existence of a rich civic network in the Twin Cities metropolitan area, which includes half the state's population.

In the late 1970s, CED studied the problems of America's cities and concluded that effective civic partnership at the local level would be critical to any meaningful solutions. In our 1982 policy statement *Public-Private Partnership: An Opportunity for Urban Communities,* we suggested some practical ways of forging such partnerships. The enormous display of energy, imagination, and cooperation at the local level over the past few years has dramatically illustrated just how much untapped potential resides in America's communities. **We believe that a large untapped civic potential resides in the fifty American states and that it can be applied to their new and challenging economic responsibilities.**

In *Public-Private Partnership,* we stressed that effective partnership

---

9. See *Public-Private Partnership: An Opportunity for Urban Communities* (New York: Committee for Economic Development, 1982).

depended on a strong civic foundation "that neither ignores nor contradicts the reality of self-interest or of political power. It simply acknowledges that individuals and political groups have a common practical interest, a civic interest, in preserving the political principles, social customs, and economic well-being of the community in which they live."[10]

---

10. This and the subsequent quotations are taken from *Public-Private Partnership: An Opportunity for Urban Communities.*

CIVIC ORGANIZATION IN MINNESOTA

Minnesota Wellspring, founded in 1981, is a public-private partnership of forty state leaders from business, government, labor, and agriculture. Its primary goals are to bring together state leaders for collaborative efforts at developing strategies to stimulate economic development. Policy proposals on specific topics, including energy, manufacturing, capital formation, and technology, are submitted to the state legislature.

Minnesota Business Partnership is a public policy advocacy association of CEOs from the largest Minnesota-based corporations. Operating strategies include identifying and analyzing long-range economic issues, creating business-government consensus, and mobilizing public opinion. Its legislative agenda for 1985 and 1986 includes reforms in taxes and expenditures, education, and unemployment compensation.

Minnesota High Technology Council, which was formed in 1982, is a nonprofit public corporation with 160 members from technology-intensive companies. The council's specific goal is to improve the business climate for technology-intensive activity, but its sole activity to date has been to improve the quality of education in the state. It also sponsors research on education and the role of technology in Minnesota's economy.

Citizens League is a nonprofit, independent civic organization. The league's primary mission is public policy research; it specializes in citizen participation that focuses on consensus building as well as policy making.

Minnesota Project is a private, nonprofit organization founded in 1979. It focuses exclusively on community economic development in rural areas. Dozens of small organizations provide technical assistance and research on statewide public policy issues pertinent to rural economies.

Spring Hill Center was formed as a nonprofit corporation in 1972. It cosponsors projects and discussions on issues important to the state. The center's principal mission is to provide a forum in which corporate and community leaders can explore solutions for social policy. Two major projects have recently focused on urban infrastructure and improving education in Minnesota.

The question we asked of urban communities is equally valid for the states: "Will the civic interest in a healthy community predominate over individual, group, or organizational interests that may be pursued, knowingly or in ignorance, to the detriment of the community?"

At the state level (as at the local level), "success in public-private relationships depends quite simply on having people who work together trust one another. With such trust, there is little that cannot be accomplished; without it, little is likely to work."

Such trust, however, must be earned. It "develops from such practical considerations as personal acquaintance among key leaders, confidence in the processes by which decisions are made and carried out, shared experience in cooperative ventures, and knowledge, through observation of past performance, of those who keep their pledges and fulfill their responsibilities. Where government is perceived as a willing partner and competent colleague, it is usually because government has, in fact, worked cooperatively and done its job well. Where the private sector is viewed as committed to the well-being of the community, it is usually because private leaders have made tangible contributions and have willingly adjusted their organizational objectives to the interests of the community."

Our optimism for state partnership is based on the same practical assessment of opportunities and motivations that formed the basis for our belief in the potential for local partnership. The opportunity arises from the fact that the "interests that bind the public and private sectors will be stronger than those that divide them." The motivation stems both from the promise of widespread benefit and from the practical realization that states failing to seize that opportunity "will lose position to those that respond more energetically."

Above all, we see in the mobilization of efforts by individual states a dynamic source of energy that can benefit the U.S. economy as a whole.

Memoranda Of Comment, Reservation, Or Dissent

Page 5, ROY L. ASH, with which HUGH M. CHAPMAN, CHARLES W. PARRY, ROCCO C. SICILIANO, and ELMER B. STAATS have asked to be associated.

A central message this statement conveys to state government leaders is that economic development is *not* merely one among many separable and delegable state government functions. State economies thrive when top state leaders — political and other — work together to determine and establish those state government policies and practices, across the whole spectrum of state activities, that are conducive to private sector innovation, efficiency, and competitiveness.

Page 34, RALPH E. BAILEY, with which ROY L. ASH has asked to be associated.

Leadership for Dynamic State Economies contains a broad and challenging overview of what I regard as a most important public policy issue, the role of states in economic development. The conclusions and recommendations of the document are sound. However, I find the study ambivalent on the most fundamental policy question: Should states attempt to be active instruments of economic change?

On the one hand, the paper clearly argues the benefits of free market reliance and reducing barriers to market efficiency and warns of pitfalls inherent in tampering with market forces. On the other hand, the study implicitly, and occasionally explicitly, advocates economic "masterminding" of the type that has states competing against one another for the same investment, without necessarily inducing new economic activity.

I firmly believe that state government must resist the temptation to intervene directly in economic decisions of the marketplace. It is certainly true that the combination of reduced federal support for state and local programs and the devastating impact of our recent recessions has put enormous pressure on state governments to "do something." The reality, however, is that state actions have not always increased the country's net investment. On a national scale, the impact of state economic development initiatives on U.S. economic activity is dominated by monetary, fiscal, and trade decisions at the federal level. States, therefore, are merely competing at the margins *with one another* for their share of new investment. Little or no net gain for the United States as a whole is attained from these programs.

At the state level, the issue is allocation of limited resources. In most cases, investment of substantial state resources in high cost, high risk economic development programs diminishes resources that could be invested in more traditional state responsibilities. Over the long term, the question is whether such economic initiatives are likely to bring greater rewards than sound fiscal management.

The major role that the states must play is ensuring a physical infrastructure and education system that is sound. Interventionist economic development programs divert needed resources from this public investment, often by a gamble against the odds and to the increasing liability of the nation.

Page 36, FRANKLIN A. LINDSAY

To resist the temptation for states to engage in escalating offers of "beggar-thy-neighbor" tax concessions in competing for a new plant's location, states should be encouraged to enter into compacts with other states renouncing or limiting such practices, akin to the treaties developed among nations to discourage unfair trade practices.

Page 52 and page 80, JAMES Q. RIORDAN

The risk that increased activity by state governments may undermine U.S. foreign policy objectives is a real one. As a case in point, states should refrain from taxing U.S. and foreign multinational businesses on a worldwide unitary basis. The unitary tax imposed by California and a few other states has soured our economic relations with the United Kingdom and other foreign governments and has exposed U.S. companies to retaliatory actions.

Page 79, HENRY B. SCHACHT

I would define tax exempt bonds issued for 501(c)(3) nonprofit tax exempt private colleges and universities and hospitals as public purpose bonds. These institutions serve essential public purposes and are the fundamental equivalent of public institutions. As such, they should be treated equally with public counterparts with respect to access to tax exempt bond financing.

Page 84, ELMER B. STAATS, with which PHILIP KLUTZNICK, CHARLES W. PARRY, and ROCCO C. SICILIANO have asked to be associated.

I believe that it would be desirable to have added to the statement the importance of interstate cooperation on a regional or national basis in the achievement of the economic objectives of individual states or regions. There are countless examples of programs in which states have joined together in furtherance of the objectives set forth in the report. Notable examples are the Delaware River Basin Commission, the New York Port Authority, and others.

As we all know, many metropolitan areas cross state boundaries which gives rise to the need for interstate cooperation for basic infrastructure requirements, such as water supply, transportation, crime control, and so forth. Growing urbanization in areas in the states from Massachusetts to Virginia on the East Coast and from San Francisco to Los Angeles to San Diego on the West Coast provides excellent illustrations of the value of coordinated planning in the transportation area. River Basin Planning Commissions established by the Congress in the early 1960s provide further examples of instances where states have joined in efforts to conserve and develop land and water resources.

There are a number of organizations at the state government level which are in a position to foster and encourage interstate cooperation, notably the National Governors Conference, the Council of State Governments, and the National Council of State Legislatures, among others. The potential for establishing a clearing house of "success stories" and evaluation of experiments undertaken by individual states in economic development and in the exchange of data could be very useful in furtherance of the objectives set forth in the excellent CED report.

Appendixes

APPENDIX A

Distribution of Tennessee, Massachusetts, and U.S. Earnings by Industries, 1983

	% of Earnings in Industry		
	United States	**Tennessee**	**Massachusetts**
Agriculture	1.75	1.15	0.66
Mining	1.66	0.58	0.05
Construction	5.30	4.78	4.16
Manufacturing	23.78	29.07	27.74
Nondurables	8.94	15.81	7.98
Food	1.86	2.38	0.95
Textiles	0.63	1.14	0.70
Apparel	0.76	2.12	0.84
Paper	0.95	1.32	1.16
Printing	1.46	1.51	1.80
Chemicals	1.71	5.00	0.86
Petroleum	0.49	0.09	0.10
Tobacco	0.12	0.13	Not Avail.
Rubber	0.81	1.53	1.11
Leather	0.15	0.59	0.45
Durables	14.84	13.26	19.77
Lumber	0.66	0.82	0.17
Furniture	0.40	0.98	0.23
Primary metals	1.37	1.29	0.61
Fabricated metals	1.76	1.86	2.03
Nonelectrical machinery	2.89	2.16	5.12
Electrical equipment	2.67	2.20	5.45
Transportation equipment (excluding cars)	1.68	0.97	1.80
Cars	1.38	0.99	0.26
Stone, clay, glass	0.73	0.94	0.52
Instruments	0.95	0.54	2.84
Miscellaneous manufactured goods	0.36	0.52	0.75

	% of Earnings in Industry		
	United States	**Tennessee**	**Massachusetts**
Transportation, communications, and utilities	7.79	7.23	6.29
Trucking and warehousing	1.65	2.58	
Utilities	1.52	0.42	
All other transport	4.62	4.23	
Wholesale trade	6.69	6.95	6.48
Retail trade	9.62	9.99	9.37
Finance, insurance, real estate	6.39	5.23	7.11
Services	20.08	18.64	24.97
Business services	3.53	2.54	4.64
Health	6.93	7.78	8.42
Legal	1.63	1.41	1.91
Educational	0.97	0.81	2.88
Social	0.58	0.30	
Other services	6.44	5.80	7.13
Government	16.97	16.39	13.18
Federal civilian	3.86	4.99	2.57
Military	1.78	0.86	0.73
State and local	11.34	10.53	9.88

SOURCE: U.S. Department of Commerce, Regional Economic Information System, as compiled in Timothy J. Bartik, "Tennessee's Economic Development: A Case Study," and Ronald Ferguson and Helen Ladd, "Economic Development in Massachusetts," prepared for the Committee for Economic Development, 1985.

APPENDIX B

State Government Actions that Affect Economic Foundations

CHART B-1

Human Resources

ELEMENT	ECONOMIC CONNECTION	ILLUSTRATIVE STATE GOVERNMENT ACTIONS
Primary and Secondary Education	Providing a skilled and adaptable work force; incentive for employees interested in their children's education.	Educational standards; teaching certification; financial assistance to local government; financial structure of local education.
Higher Education	Providing a higher-level skilled work force; attraction of teaching/research talent; inducement to industry reliant on research and graduate education.	Support for universities and community colleges.
Labor Market-Adjustment	Retraining work force; adapting skills for changing labor market; adjustment assistance for shift to other employment.	Vocational education through secondary schools and community colleges. Job service and Job Training Partnership Act through local Private Industry Councils; employment service; unemployment insurance; public assistance.
Health	Helping employees remain productive; health care a major cost of business.	Health industry regulation; workers' compensation; occupational health and safety.
Human Services	Helping employees remain productive; quality of life.	Income maintenance; housing assistance.
Labor Relations	Employee rights and nature of labor management.	Regulation of labor-management relations.

CHART B-2
Physical Infrastructure

ELEMENT	ECONOMIC CONNECTION	ILLUSTRATIVE STATE GOVERNMENT ACTIONS
Transportation	Basic system of roads, bridges, tunnels, ports, airports, and mass transit required for commerce and personal movement for business purposes.	Building, maintenance, and operation of highway system, ports, airports; determination of local ability to provide transportation infrastructure.
Water Supply and Sewerage	Water supply required for industrial and population growth. Water quality required for health and environmental purposes; important to water-related industry (fisheries, recreation) and to quality of life.	Regulation of local government provision of water and sewer facilities; building and operation of water and sewer systems.
Waste Management	Solid waste collection and disposal required for industrial and population growth and quality of life.	Regulation of local government disposal of solid waste; building and operation of disposal systems.
Communication	Telecommunications.	Regulation of telephone companies; determination of local authority for cable television.
Energy	Gas and electric utilities required for industry, business, and consumers.	Regulation of gas and electric utilities; determination of local government structure for municipal energy utilities.
Housing	Housing required for all citizens; itself a key industry.	Regulation of housing code and permits.

CHART B-3
Natural Resources

ELEMENT	ECONOMIC CONNECTION	ILLUSTRATIVE STATE GOVERNMENT ACTIONS
Land	Space requirements for economic activity, opportunity costs in other uses foregone. Land resources have economic value (e.g., soil, minerals, forests, watersheds, recreation, etc.).	Regional land use planning and regulation; determination of local land use regulation; balancing the economic uses of land. Geographic location strategies.
Water	Lakes, rivers, streams, and ground water provide water supply for industry and population growth; fisheries and recreational industry.	Regulation and development of water resources. Promotion of tourism and water-related industry.
Air	Clean air required for health and quality of life.	Air quality regulation.
Agriculture	Agriculture is a key industry in several states.	Land regulation, farm assistance; cooperative extension service; rural development programs; agricultural preservation programs.
Minerals	Oil, coal, and hard metals mining are key industries in several states.	Regulation of mining; assistance to mining firms; research to promote mineral resource use; provision of infrastructure required for exploitation; conservation management.
Forests	Forestry products are key industries in many states; also recreation, tourism, quality of life.	Forest management; protection for recreational uses.
Wildlife	Wildlife is important for quality of life and some industry.	Regulation, conservation, development.

CHART B-4

Knowledge and Technology

ELEMENT	ECONOMIC CONNECTION	ILLUSTRATIVE STATE GOVERNMENT ACTIONS
Information	Basic economic information important both to business and to job seekers. Generation and dissemination of information itself a major economic activity.	Provision of economic information; operation of or support for local libraries; promotion of information exchange and networks.
Research and Development	Research and development is a prime source of new technology.	Support of university research and centers of applied research in areas critical to state industry.
Universities	University research, development, dissemination and application of new knowledge and technology important to economic growth.	Support of universities; development of strength in key areas of research.
Linkages Between Universities, Research, and Business	Basic and applied research important to development of new technologies and their commercial application. University-business connection for research, development, commercial application, and continuing education is now an important economic function.	Support for linkages among existing research centers and business, or creation of new institutions; promotion of new technologies.

CHART B-5
Enterprise Development

ELEMENT	ECONOMIC CONNECTION	ILLUSTRATIVE STATE GOVERNMENT ACTIONS
Promotion	Knowledge of a state's business potential encourages investment; knowledge of a state's products helps sales.	Advertising, mailings, information, trade fairs, personal visits, out-of-state offices, export promotion.
Capital Markets	Availability of capital is critical to business starts and expansion.	Regulation of capital markets; increasing availability of capital for enterprise.
Financial Assistance	Special financial assistance may provide incentive or support for firms that otherwise would not start, expand, continue, or locate in the state.	Administration of federal programs (IRB, SBA 7a, SBA 503, UDAG, CDBG, Section 208); tax abatements, loans, loan guarantees, grants.
Regulation	Protect markets from anti-competitive practices; protect consumers from unsafe products; protect businesses from unfair practices; protect public health, safety, and welfare.	Regulation of anti-trust, consumer protection, unfair business practices, public health, safety, and welfare; professions, trades; banking, insurance, land use.
Special Life Cycle Needs of Firms	Firms have special needs in starting, expanding, maturing, dematuring, declining, contracting, closing, and relocating.	Technical or financial assistance to help firms in these stages.

CHART B-6
Quality of Life

ELEMENT	ECONOMIC CONNECTION	ILLUSTRATIVE STATE GOVERNMENT ACTIONS
Cost of Living	Cost of living is a function of the cost of doing business, which is in turn affected by state actions.	Consideration of effect of state actions on the cost of doing business.
Job Availability and Wage Levels	Jobs and wage levels are a function of economic activity.	Promotion of healthy economic environment.
Physical Environment	Workers and businesses seek a satisfactory place to live and work.	Promotion and protection of the living and working environment.
Goods and Services	Workers and businesses seek a place to live and work where both public and private goods and services are available.	Promotion of a vibrant private economy and provision of public services.
Amenities	Workers and businesses seek such amenities as open space, recreational facilities, sports, cultural activities, etc.	Provision of amenities; or other promotion and encouragement of private provision of amenities.
Community	Workers and businesses seek a sense of community through public participation, political involvement, and honest government.	Promotion of a sense of community by encouraging public participation and strong civic institutions.

CHART B-7
Fiscal Management

ELEMENT	ECONOMIC CONNECTION	ILLUSTRATIVE STATE GOVERNMENT ACTIONS
General Tax Levels	High personal taxes are a disincentive to employees and managers.	Determining tax rates and relative share of income, sales, property, and other taxes, as well as fees and other revenue sources; consideration of impact on state competitiveness.
Business Taxes and Fees	High business taxes add to business costs and increase prices of goods and services.	Determining business taxes and fees, consideration of effect on state competitiveness and impact on business costs.
Tax Expenditures and Subsidies	Tax abatements and subsidies may or may not generate compensating revenue.	Assessment of net fiscal impact of tax abatements and subsidies.
Debt	State debt affects tax rates and financing infrastructure.	Debt management for fiscal stability and soundness and infrastructure.
Other Costs	Tax savings from inadequate public services may impose costs on business (e.g., maintenance of vehicles due to poor roads, remedial training for public school graduates).	Assessment of real costs and fiscal impacts of public policy and service levels.

APPENDIX C

The Evolution of Economic Development Agencies

Publications dealing with state issues and governor's state-of-the-state messages continue to distinguish between "economic development" programs and those dealing with education, agriculture, natural resources, energy, transportation, labor, income security, and other areas that are of central economic importance to the state. This conventional use of "economic development" can be traced to early government programs designed to strengthen regional economies by recruiting manufacturing plants.

In the 1930s, nearly every state established an office of state planning, mainly at the prompting of the federal government, to work with the National Resources Planning Board and the Works Progress Administration. A few states also established industrial development agencies at their own initiative to recruit branch manufacturing plants or encourage tourism.

Nearly all of the planning agencies were abolished during World War II when the federal government stopped funding them, and the economic recovery associated with the war effort made them seem unnecessary. A few industrial development agencies, however, were continued, and following World War II, other states fearing recession established similar agencies.

In 1954, the federal government revived its interest in sub-national planning through its "701" program, but it first focused attention on local governments. Grants were provided to state industrial development agencies to assist local governments in improving their planning. The program was extended to state planning in 1961, and, by 1975, every state once again had a state planning agency. Meanwhile, an increasing number of states created economic development departments in the mode of the forerunner industrial development agencies. Some were combined with community development departments which were created in the 1950s to consolidate programs — mainly federal grants — dealing with local government.

Today, agencies designated as responsible for economic development, variously called departments of commerce, industry, or industrial development, vary widely in organization.[1] Some, such as those in Connecticut,

---

1. Council of State Governments, *Economic Development: A Survey of State Activities*, Lexington, Kentucky; 1983; and Thomas J. Anton and Rebecca Reynolds, "Old Federalism and New Policies for State Economic Development," A. Alfred Taubman Center for Public Policy and American Institutions, Brown University, 1985. Three states — Alabama, Connecticut, and Pennsylvania — established their departments in the 1930s; seven were established in the 40s; twelve in the 50s; thirteen in the 60s; eight in the 70s; and seven since 1980.

Rhode Island, and Tennessee, have expanded to incorporate new responsibilities for technology-related industry while remaining the lead agency in economic policy development. Some have continued to perform the traditional economic functions while other agencies, or newly created agencies, have taken on responsibilities for newer economic programs, or for related functions such as job training, housing, and community development.

Simple steps could be taken to remove part of the confusion. For example, economic affairs could be considered a staff activity of the governor, similar to the budget and finance responsibilities, with no line agency bearing the formal "economic development" label. Agencies which deal in such matters as promotion, business development, and technical assistance, would more appropriately be called "enterprise development" which represents only one element of the state's economic program.

Examples of other forms include the following:

- In Indiana, the Department of Commerce is headed by the lieutenant governor. An Employment and Development Commission was created in 1982 with the power to issue bonds in order to lend money and create jobs.

- Minnesota has a Department of Energy and Economic Development, a Department of Commerce, and a Governor's Office of Science and Technology.

- South Dakota has a Bureau of Industrial and Agriculture Development, and a Department of Tourism and Commerce, having eliminated the Department of Economic and Tourist Development in 1981.

- Montana created an Economic Development Board in 1983 to implement a statewide economic development program required by a 1983 voter initiative.

- Maryland, which created a cabinet-level Department of Employment and Training in 1983, also has a Department of Economic and Community Development.

Following is a list of the research papers prepared as background for the CED Subcommittee on State Economic Progress. These papers will be published in a separate volume.

Tennessee's Economic Development: A Case Study
Timothy J. Bartik, Assistant Professor of Economics,
Department of Economics and Business Administration
Vanderbilt University

Economic Performance and Economic Development Policy in Massachusetts
Ronald F. Ferguson, Assistant Professor of Public Policy
John F. Kennedy School of Government, Harvard University
Helen F. Ladd, Professor of Public Policy
Duke University

California: Inventing the Future through Investment and Innovation
Douglas Henton, Senior Policy Analyst
SRI International
Steven A. Waldhorn, Director, Public Policy Center
SRI International

Economic Development in Michigan: Choosing an Economic Future
John E. Jackson, Professor of Political Science and
  Program Director, Center for Political Studies
Institute for Social Research
The University of Michigan

A Quality Public Sector as a Strategy for Economic Growth
Ted Kolderie, Senior Fellow,
Hubert H. Humphrey Institute of Public Affairs
University of Minnesota
William A. Blazar, Public Policy Consultant

Arizona: A Case Study
Larry Landry, President
Landry & Associates

Economic Development in Indiana: A Strategic Step
Charles R. Warren
Indiana University

OBJECTIVES OF THE COMMITTEE FOR ECONOMIC DEVELOPMENT

For over forty years, the Committee for Economic Development has been a respected influence on the formation of business and public policy. CED is devoted to these two objectives:

To develop, through objective research and informed discussion, findings and recommendations for private and public policy that will contribute to preserving and strengthening our free society, achieving steady economic growth at high employment and reasonably stable prices, increasing productivity and living standards, providing greater and more equal opportunity for every citizen, and improving the quality of life for all.

To bring about increasing understanding by present and future leaders in business, government, and education, and among concerned citizens, of the importance of these objectives and the ways in which they can be achieved.

CED's work is supported strictly by private voluntary contributions from business and industry, foundations, and individuals. It is independent, nonprofit, nonpartisan, and nonpolitical.

The two hundred trustees, who generally are presidents or board chairmen of corporations and presidents of universities, are chosen for their individual capacities rather than as representatives of any particular interests. By working with scholars, they unite business judgment and experience with scholarship in analyzing the issues and developing recommendations to resolve the economic problems that constantly arise in a dynamic and democratic society.

Through this business-academic partnership, CED endeavors to develop policy statements and other research materials that commend themselves as guides to public and business policy; that can be used as texts in college economics and political science courses and in management training courses; that will be considered and discussed by newspaper and magazine editors, columnists, and commentators; and that are distributed abroad to promote better understanding of the American economic system.

CED believes that by enabling businessmen to demonstrate constructively their concern for the general welfare, it is helping business to earn and maintain the national and community respect essential to the successful functioning of the free enterprise capitalist system.

CED BOARD OF TRUSTEES

Chairman
EDMUND B. FITZGERALD, Chairman and Chief
 Executive Officer
Northern Telecom Limited

Vice Chairmen
OWEN B. BUTLER, Retired Chairman
The Procter & Gamble Company

WILLIAM S. EDGERLY, Chairman
State Street Bank and Trust Company

PHILIP M. HAWLEY, Chairman of the Board
Carter Hawley Hale Stores, Inc.

JAMES L. KETELSEN, Chairman and Chief Executive
 Officer
Tenneco Inc.

FRANKLIN A. LINDSAY, Chairman
Vectron, Inc.

WILLIAM S. WOODSIDE, Chairman
American Can Company

Treasurer
JOHN B. CAVE
Summit, New Jersey

EDWARD L. ADDISON, President
The Southern Company

HOWARD P. ALLEN, Chairman and Chief Executive
 Officer
Southern California Edison Company

ROY L. ASH
Los Angeles, California

H. B. ATWATER, JR., Chairman of the Board and Chief
 Executive Officer
General Mills, Inc.

RALPH E. BAILEY, Chairman and Chief Executive
 Officer
Conoco Inc.

ROBERT H. B. BALDWIN, Chairman, Advisory Board
Morgan Stanley & Co. Incorporated

J. DAVID BARNES, Chairman and Chief Executive
 Officer
Mellon Bank N.A.

Z. E. BARNES, Chairman and Chief Executive Officer
Southwestern Bell Corporation

JAMES K. BATTEN, President
Knight-Ridder Newspapers, Inc.

WARREN L. BATTS, President
Dart & Kraft, Inc.

ROBERT A. BECK, Chairman and Chief Executive
 Officer
The Prudential Insurance Company of America

JACK F. BENNETT, Senior Vice President
Exxon Corporation

JAMES F. BERÉ, Chairman
Borg-Warner Corporation

DEREK C. BOK, President
Harvard University

JOAN T. BOK, Chairman
New England Electric System

ALAN S. BOYD, Chairman
Airbus Industrie of North America

JOHN BRADEMAS, President
New York University

WILLIAM H. BRICKER, Chairman, President and Chief
 Executive Officer
Diamond Shamrock Corporation

ANDREW F. BRIMMER, President
Brimmer & Company, Inc.

ALFRED BRITTAIN III, Chairman of the Board
Bankers Trust Company

PERRY G. BRITTAIN, Chairman of the Board and Chief
 Executive Officer
Texas Utilities Company

CEES BRUYNES, Chairman, President and Chief
 Executive Officer
North American Philips Corporation

JOHN H. BRYAN, JR., Chairman and Chief Executive
 Officer
Sara Lee Corporation

MICHAEL H. BULKIN, Director
McKinsey & Company, Inc.

THEODORE A. BURTIS, Chairman of the Board
Sun Company, Inc.

OWEN B. BUTLER, Retired Chairman
The Procter & Gamble Company

*FLETCHER L. BYROM, Retired Chairman
Koppers Company, Inc.

PHILIP A. CAMPBELL, President
Bell Atlantic Network Services, Inc.

ROBERT J. CARLSON, Chairman, President and Chief
 Executive Officer
BMC Industries Inc.

RAFAEL CARRION, JR., Chairman of the Board
Banco Popular de Puerto Rico

EDWARD M. CARSON, President
First Interstate Bancorp

R. E. CARTLEDGE, Chairman, President and Chief
 Executive Officer
Union Camp Corporation

JOHN B. CAVE
Summit, New Jersey

HUGH M. CHAPMAN, President
The Citizens and Southern Corporation

ROBERT A. CHARPIE, President
Cabot Corporation

ROBERT CIZIK, Chairman and President
Cooper Industries, Inc.

DAVID R. CLARE, President
Johnson & Johnson

DONALD C. CLARK, Chairman of the Board and Chief
 Executive Officer
Household International

ROBERT B. CLAYTOR, Chairman and Chief Executive
 Officer
Norfolk Southern Corporation

*Life Trustee

W. GRAHAM CLAYTOR, JR., Chairman and President
Amtrak

JOHN L. CLENDENIN, Chairman of the Board
BellSouth Corporation

*EMILIO G. COLLADO, Executive Chairman
International Planning Corporation

ROBERT L. CRANDALL, Chairman and President
American Airlines

THOMAS H. CRUIKSHANK, President and Chief
    Executive Officer
Halliburton Company

DOUGLAS D. DANFORTH, Chairman
Westinghouse Electric Corporation

RONALD R. DAVENPORT, Chairman of the Board
Sheridan Broadcasting Corporation

RALPH P. DAVIDSON, Chairman of the Board
Time Inc.

MARTIN S. DAVIS, Chairman and Chief Executive
    Officer
Gulf+Western Inc.

BARBARA K. DEBS, Corporate Director
Greenwich, Connecticut

ALFRED C. DECRANE, JR., President
Texaco Inc.

ROBERT W. DECHERD, President and Chief Operating
    Officer
A. H. Belo Corporation

ROBERT F. DEE, Chairman of the Board
SmithKline Beckman Corporation

WILLIAM N. DERAMUS III, Chairman
Kansas City Southern Industries, Inc.

PETER A. DEROW, President
CBS/Publishing Group
CBS Inc.

JOHN DIEBOLD, Chairman
The Diebold Group, Inc.

GEORGE C. DILLON, Chairman of the Board
Butler Manufacturing Company

ROBERT R. DOCKSON, Chairman of the Board
CalFed Inc.

EDWIN D. DODD, Chairman Emeritus
Owens-Illinois, Inc.

JOHN T. DORRANCE, JR., Chairman of the Executive
    Committee
Campbell Soup Company

FRANK P. DOYLE, Senior Vice President
General Electric Company

W. D. EBERLE, President
Manchester Associates, Ltd.

WILLIAM S. EDGERLY, Chairman
State Street Bank and Trust Company

JOHN R. EDMAN, Vice President
General Motors Corporation

ROBERT F. ERBURU, Chairman and Chief Executive
    Officer
The Times Mirror Company

WILLIAM T. ESREY, President and Chief Executive
    Officer
United Telecommunications, Inc.

J. LEE EVERETT III, Chairman and Chief Executive
    Officer
Philadelphia Electric Company

LYLE EVERINGHAM, Chairman of the Board and Chief
    Executive Officer
The Kroger Co.

THOMAS J. EYERMAN, Partner
Skidmore, Owings & Merrill

JAMES B. FARLEY, Senior Chairman
Booz·Allen & Hamilton Inc.

DAVID C. FARRELL, Chairman and Chief Executive
    Officer
The May Department Stores Company

JOHN H. FILER, Partner
Tyler, Cooper & Alcorn

EDMUND B. FITZGERALD, Chairman and Chief
    Executive Officer
Northern Telecom Limited

JOSEPH B. FLAVIN, Chairman and Chief Executive
    Officer
The Singer Company

PETER H. FORSTER, President and Chief Executive
    Officer
Dayton Power and Light Company

*WILLIAM H. FRANKLIN, Chairman of the Board,
    Retired
Caterpillar Tractor Co.

ROBERT R. FREDERICK, President and Chief Executive
    Officer
RCA Corporation

HARRY L. FREEMAN, Executive Vice President,
    Corporate Affairs and Communications
American Express Company

THOMAS F. FRIST, JR., M.D., Chairman and Chief
    Executive Officer
Hospital Corporation of America

ROBERT F. FROEHLKE, Chairman of the Board
Equitable Life Assurance Society of the United States

GERALD W. FRONTERHOUSE, Chairman and Chief
    Executive Officer
RepublicBank Corporation

H. LAURANCE FULLER, President
Amoco Corporation

DONALD E. GARRETSON, Community Service
    Executive Program
3M Company

CLIFTON C. GARVIN, JR., Chairman of the Board
Exxon Corporation

RICHARD L. GELB, Chairman and Chief Executive
    Officer
Bristol-Myers Company

JOHN A. GEORGES, Chairman and Chief Executive
    Officer
International Paper Co.

WALTER B. GERKEN, Chairman of the Board
Pacific Mutual Life Insurance Company

PIERRE GOUSSELAND, Honorary Chairman
AMAX Inc.

THOMAS C. GRAHAM, President
USS Inc.

EARL G. GRAVES, President
Earl G. Graves Ltd.

HANNA H. GRAY, President
University of Chicago

W. GRANT GREGORY, Chairman of the Board
Touche Ross & Co.

DAVID L. GROVE, President
David L. Grove, Ltd.

CLIFFORD J. GRUM, President and Chief Executive
    Officer
Temple-Inland Inc.

*Life Trustee

DONALD E. GUINN, Chairman and Chief Executive
  Officer
Pacific Telesis Group

JOHN H. GUTFREUND, Chairman and Chief Executive
  Officer
Salomon Inc

BRENTON S. HALSEY, Chairman and Chief Executive
  Officer
James River Corporation

RICHARD P. HAMILTON, Chairman and Chief
  Executive Officer
Hartmarx Corp.

RICHARD W. HANSELMAN, Former Chairman
Genesco Inc.

ROBERT A. HANSON, Chairman and Chief Executive
  Officer
Deere & Company

PAUL HARDIN, President
Drew University

CHARLES M. HARPER, Chairman of the Board and
  Chief Executive Officer
ConAgra, Inc.

FRED L. HARTLEY, Chairman and Chief Executive
  Officer
Unocal Corporation

ROBERT J. HAUGH, Chairman and Chief Executive
  Officer
The St. Paul Companies, Inc.

BARBARA B. HAUPTFUHRER, Corporate Director
Huntingdon Valley, Pennsylvania

ARTHUR HAUSPURG, Chairman of the Board
Consolidated Edison Company of New York, Inc.

PHILIP M. HAWLEY, Chairman of the Board
Carter Hawley Hale Stores, Inc.

RAYMOND A. HAY, Chairman and Chief Executive
  Officer
The LTV Corporation

HAROLD W. HAYNES, Executive Vice President and
  Chief Financial Officer
The Boeing Company

RALPH L. HENNEBACH, Retired Chairman
ASARCO Incorporated

LAWRENCE HICKEY, Chairman
Stein Roe & Farnham

RODERICK M. HILLS, Distinguished Faculty Fellow
  and Lecturer
Yale University School of Organization and
  Management

ROBERT C. HOLLAND, President
Committee for Economic Development

LEON C. HOLT, JR., Vice Chairman and Chief
  Administrative Officer
Air Products and Chemicals, Inc.

ROBERT B. HORTON, Chairman and Chief Executive
  Officer
The Standard Oil Company

JAMES R. HOUGHTON, Chairman and Chief
  Executive Officer
Corning Glass Works

ROY M. HUFFINGTON, Chairman of the Board
Roy M. Huffington, Inc.

WILLIAM S. KANAGA, Chairman, Advisory Board
Arthur Young

JOSEPH E. KASPUTYS, Executive Vice President,
  Development
McGraw-Hill, Inc.

DAVID T. KEARNS, Chairman and Chief Executive
  Officer
Xerox Corporation

GEORGE M. KELLER, Chairman of the Board
Chevron Corporation

DONALD P. KELLY, Chairman and Chief Executive
  Officer
Beatrice Companies, Inc.

JAMES M. KEMPER, JR., Chairman of the Board
Commerce Bancshares, Inc.

J. C. KENEFICK, Vice Chairman
Union Pacific Corporation

GEORGE D. KENNEDY, President and Chief Executive
  Officer
International Minerals and Chemical Corporation

JAMES L. KETELSEN, Chairman and Chief Executive
  Officer
Tenneco Inc.

ROBERT D. KILPATRICK, Chairman and Chief
  Executive Officer
CIGNA Corporation

CHARLES M. KITTRELL, Executive Vice President
Phillips Petroleum Company

PHILIP M. KLUTZNICK, Senior Partner
Klutznick Investments

CHARLES F. KNIGHT, Chairman and Chief Executive
  Officer
Emerson Electric Co.

WILLIAM E. LAMOTHE, Chairman and Chief Executive
  Officer
Kellogg Company

RALPH LAZARUS, Chairman Emeritus
Federated Department Stores, Inc.

DREW LEWIS, Chairman and Chief Executive Officer
Union Pacific Railroad Company

FLOYD W. LEWIS, Retired Chairman
Middle South Utilities, Inc.

FRANKLIN A. LINDSAY, Chairman
Vectron, Inc.

FRANCIS P. LUCIER
Mohawk Data Sciences Corporation

JACK A. MACALLISTER, Chairman and Chief Executive
  Officer
U S WEST, Inc.

BRUCE K. MACLAURY, President
The Brookings Institution

COLETTE MAHONEY, RSHM, President
Marymount Manhattan College

WILLIAM A. MARQUARD, Consultant
American Standard Inc.

DONALD B. MARRON, Chairman, President and Chief
  Executive Officer
PaineWebber Group Inc.

WILLIAM F. MAY, President
Statue of Liberty — Ellis Island Foundation, Inc.

JEWELL JACKSON MCCABE, President
The National Coalition of 100 Black Women

HOWARD C. MCCRADY, Chairman and Chief
  Executive Officer
Valley National Corporation

ALONZO L. MCDONALD, Chairman and Chief
  Executive Officer
Avenir Group, Inc.

JOHN F. MCGILLICUDDY, Chairman of the Board and
  Chief Executive Officer
Manufacturers Hanover Corporation

JAMES W. MCKEE, JR., Chairman
CPC International Inc.

JOHN A. MCKINNEY, Chairman of the Board and Chief
    Executive Officer
Manville Corporation

ROBERT E. MERCER, Chairman of the Board
The Goodyear Tire & Rubber Company

RUBEN F. METTLER, Chairman of the Board and Chief
    Executive Officer
TRW Inc.

GEORGE F. MOODY, President and Chief Executive
    Officer
Security Pacific National Bank

STEVEN MULLER, President
The Johns Hopkins University

JOSEPH NEUBAUER, Chairman, President and Chief
    Executive Officer
ARA Services, Inc.

BARBARA W. NEWELL, Lecturer on Education
Harvard University

EDWARD N. NEY, Chairman of the Board
Young & Rubicam Inc.

JAMES J. O'CONNOR, Chairman and President
Commonwealth Edison Company

WILLIAM S. OGDEN, Chairman and Chief Executive
    Officer
Continental Illinois National Bank and Trust Company
    of Chicago

LEIF H. OLSEN, President
Leif H. Olsen Associates, Inc.

JOHN D. ONG, Chairman of the Board
The BFGoodrich Company

ANTHONY J. F. O'REILLY, President and Chief
    Executive Officer
H.J. Heinz Company

RICHARD de J. OSBORNE, Chairman, President and
    Chief Executive Officer
ASARCO Inc.

NORMA PACE, Senior Vice President
American Paper Institute

ALCESTE T. PAPPAS, Principal
Peat Marwick Mitchell and Co.

CHARLES W. PARRY, Chairman and Chief Executive
    Officer
Aluminum Company of America

PETER G. PETERSON, Chairman
The Blackstone Group

JOHN J. PHELAN, JR., Chairman and Chief Executive
    Officer
New York Stock Exchange, Inc.

EDWARD E. PHILLIPS, Chairman and Chief Executive
    Officer
The New England

DEAN P. PHYPERS, Senior Vice President
IBM Corporation

HAROLD A. POLING, President
Ford Motor Company

EDMUND T. PRATT, JR., Chairman of the Board and
    Chief Executive Officer
Pfizer Inc.

LELAND S. PRUSSIA, Chairman of the Board
BankAmerica Corporation

JOHN R. PURCELL, Chairman and President
SFN Companies, Inc.

ALLAN L. RAYFIELD, President and Chief Operating
    Officer
Diversified Products and Services Group
GTE Service Corporation

JAMES J. RENIER, President
Honeywell Inc.

FRANK H. T. RHODES, President
Cornell University

JAMES Q. RIORDAN, Vice Chairman and Chief
    Financial Officer
Mobil Corporation

BURNELL R. ROBERTS, Chairman and Chief Executive
    Officer
The Mead Corporation

IAN M. ROLLAND, Chairman
Lincoln National Life Insurance Company

FRANCIS C. ROONEY, JR., Chairman of the Board
Melville Corporation

DONALD K. ROSS, Chairman of the Board
New York Life Insurance Company

THOMAS F. RUSSELL, Chairman and Chief Executive
    Officer
Federal-Mogul Corporation

JOHN SAGAN, Retired Vice President - Treasurer
Ford Motor Company

VINCENT A. SARNI, Chairman and Chief Executive
    Officer
PPG Industries, Inc.

RALPH S. SAUL, Financial Consultant
Philadelphia, Pennsylvania

HENRY B. SCHACHT, Chairman of the Board and Chief
    Executive Officer
Cummins Engine Company, Inc.

ROBERT M. SCHAEBERLE, Chairman
Nabisco Brands Inc.

GEORGE A. SCHAEFER, Chairman and Chief Executive
    Officer
Caterpillar Tractor Co.

ROBERT A. SCHOELLHORN, Chairman and Chief
    Executive Officer
Abbott Laboratories

WILLIAM A. SCHREYER, Chairman and Chief
    Executive Officer
Merrill Lynch & Co. Inc.

DONALD J. SCHUENKE, President and Chief Executive
    Officer
Northwestern Mutual Life Insurance Company

ROBERT G. SCHWARTZ, Chairman of the Board
Metropolitan Life Insurance Company

J. L. SCOTT, Chairman
J. L. Scott Enterprises, Inc.

S. F. SEGNAR, Retired Chairman
HNG/InterNorth, Inc.

DONNA E. SHALALA, President
Hunter College

MARK SHEPHERD, JR., Chairman
Texas Instruments Incorporated

WALTER V. SHIPLEY, Chairman and Chief Executive
    Officer
Chemical Bank

ROCCO C. SICILIANO, Of Counsel
Jones, Day, Reavis & Pogue

ANDREW C. SIGLER, Chairman and Chief Executive
    Officer
Champion International Corporation

*Life Trustee

RICHARD D. SIMMONS, President
The Washington Post Company

L. EDWIN SMART, Chairman of the Board
Transworld Corporation

FREDERICK W. SMITH, Chairman and Chief Executive
  Officer
Federal Express Corporation

PHILIP L. SMITH, President and Chief Operating
  Officer
General Foods Corporation

ROGER B. SMITH, Chairman
General Motors Corporation

SHERWOOD H. SMITH, JR., Chairman and President
Carolina Power & Light Company

TIMOTHY P. SMUCKER, President and Chief
  Operating Officer
The J. M. Smucker Company

ELMER B. STAATS, Former Comptroller General of the
  United States
Washington, D.C.

JOHN M. STAFFORD, Chairman, President and Chief
  Executive Officer
The Pillsbury Company

DELBERT C. STALEY, Chairman and Chief Executive
  Officer
NYNEX Corporation

GORDON K. G. STEVENS, Chairman and Chief
  Executive Officer
Unilever United States, Inc.

DONALD M. STEWART, President
Spelman College

WILLIAM P. STIRITZ, Chairman of the Board
Ralston Purina Company

*WILLIAM C. STOLK,
Bridgeport, Connecticut

BARRY F. SULLIVAN, Chairman of the Board
First National Bank of Chicago

MORRIS TANENBAUM, Executive Vice President
AT&T

G. J. TANKERSLEY, Chairman
Consolidated Natural Gas Company

DAVID S. TAPPAN, JR., Chairman and Chief Executive
  Officer
Fluor Corporation

EDWARD R. TELLING, Chairman of the Board
The Saving & Profit Sharing Fund of Sears Employees
Sears, Roebuck and Co.

JOSEPH G. TEMPLE, JR., Executive Vice President
The Dow Chemical Company

ANTHONY P. TERRACCIANO, Vice Chairman, Global
  Banking
The Chase Manhattan Bank, N.A.

WALTER N. THAYER, Chairman
Whitney Communications Company

W. BRUCE THOMAS, Vice Chairman of
  Administration and Chief Financial Officer
USX Corporation

THOMAS A. VANDERSLICE, Chairman, President and
  Chief Executive Officer
Apollo Computer Inc.

ALVA O. WAY, Chairman
J. Henry Schroder Bank & Trust

ARNOLD R. WEBER, President
Northwestern University

SIDNEY J. WEINBERG, JR., Partner
Goldman, Sachs & Co.

K. M. WEIS, President and Chief Executive Officer
Bayer USA Inc.

WALTER L. WEISMAN, President and Chief Executive
  Officer
American Medical International Inc.

WILLIAM L. WEISS, Chairman and Chief Executive
  Officer
Ameritech

JOHN F. WELCH, JR., Chairman and Chief Executive
  Officer
General Electric Company

CLIFTON R. WHARTON, JR., Chancellor
State University of New York

DOLORES D. WHARTON, President
The Fund for Corporate Initiatives, Inc.

HAROLD M. WILLIAMS, President
The J. Paul Getty Trust

J. KELLEY WILLIAMS, President
First Mississippi Corporation

JOSEPH D. WILLIAMS, Chairman and Chief Executive
  Officer
Warner-Lambert Company

THOMAS R. WILLIAMS, Chairman
First Wachovia Corporation

*W. WALTER WILLIAMS
Seattle, Washington

J. TYLEE WILSON, Chairman and Chief Executive
  Officer
RJR Nabisco

MARGARET S. WILSON, Chairman of the Board
Scarbroughs

RICHARD D. WOOD, Chairman, President and Chief
  Executive Officer
Eli Lilly and Company

WILLIAM S. WOODSIDE, Chairman
American Can Company

M. CABELL WOODWARD, JR., Vice Chairman and
  Chief Financial Officer
ITT Corporation

CHARLES J. ZWICK, Chairman and Chief Executive
  Officer
Southeast Banking Corporation

HONORARY TRUSTEES

RAY C. ADAM, Retired Chairman
NL Industries, Inc.

E. SHERMAN ADAMS
New Preston, Connecticut

CARL E. ALLEN
North Muskegon, Michigan

JAMES L. ALLEN, Honorary Chairman
Booz•Allen & Hamilton Inc.

O. KELLEY ANDERSON
Boston, Massachusetts

ROBERT O. ANDERSON, Director and
    Chairman, Executive Committee
Atlantic Richfield Company

SANFORD S. ATWOOD
Lake Toxaway, North Carolina

JOSEPH W. BARR, Corporate Director
Arlington, Virginia

HARRY HOOD BASSETT, Chairman, Executive
    Committee
Southeast Bank N.A.

S. CLARK BEISE, President (Retired)
Bank of America N.T. & S.A.

GEORGE F. BENNETT, President
State Street Research & Management Company

HAROLD H. BENNETT
Salt Lake City, Utah

HOWARD W. BLAUVELT
Charlottesville, Virginia

JOSEPH L. BLOCK, Former Chairman
Inland Steel Company

FRED J. BORCH
New Canaan, Connecticut

MARVIN BOWER
McKinsey & Company, Inc.

JOHN L. BURNS, President
John L. Burns and Company

THOMAS D. CABOT, Honorary Chairman of the Board
Cabot Corporation

ALEXANDER CALDER, JR., Chairman, Executive
    Committee
Union Camp Corporation

PHILIP CALDWELL, Senior Managing Director
Shearson Lehman Brothers Inc.

EDWARD W. CARTER, Chairman Emeritus
Carter Hawley Hale Stores, Inc.

EVERETT N. CASE
Van Hornesville, New York

HUNG WO CHING, Chairman of the Board
Aloha Airlines, Inc.

WALKER L. CISLER
Overseas Advisory Service
Detroit, Michigan

ROBERT C. COSGROVE
Naples, Florida

GEORGE S. CRAFT
Atlanta, Georgia

JOHN H. DANIELS, Retired Chairman
National City Bancorporation

ARCHIE K. DAVIS, Chairman of the Board (Retired)
Wachovia Bank and Trust Company, N.A.

DONALD C. DAYTON, Director
Dayton Hudson Corporation

DOUGLAS DILLON, Chairman, Executive Committee
Dillon, Read and Co. Inc.

ALFRED W. EAMES, JR., Retired Chairman
Del Monte Corporation

FRANCIS E. FERGUSON, Retired Chairman of the
    Board
Northwestern Mutual Life Insurance Company

JOHN T. FEY
Stowe, Vermont

WILLIAM S. FISHMAN, Chairman, Executive
    Committee
ARA Services, Inc.

JOHN M. FOX
Orlando, Florida

GAYLORD FREEMAN
Chicago, Illinois

DON C. FRISBEE, Chairman
PacifiCorp

W. H. KROME GEORGE, Chairman, Executive
    Committee
Aluminum Company of America

PAUL S. GEROT, Honorary Chairman of the Board
The Pillsbury Company

LINCOLN GORDON, Guest Scholar
The Brookings Institution

KATHARINE GRAHAM, Chairman
The Washington Post Company

JOHN D. GRAY, Chairman Emeritus
Hartmarx Corp.

WILLIAM C. GREENOUGH, Retired Chairman
TIAA and CREF

WALTER A. HAAS, JR., Honorary Chairman of the
    Board
Levi Strauss and Co.

MICHAEL L. HAIDER
New York, New York

TERRANCE HANOLD
Edina, Minnesota

ROBERT S. HATFIELD
New York, New York

H. J. HEINZ II, Chairman
H. J. Heinz Company

J. V. HERD, Director
The Continental Insurance Companies

OVETA CULP HOBBY, Chairman
H & C Communications, Inc.

GEORGE F. JAMES
South Bristol, Maine

HENRY R. JOHNSTON
Ponte Vedra Beach, Florida

GILBERT E. JONES, Retired Vice Chairman
IBM Corporation

FREDERICK R. KAPPEL
Sarasota, Florida

CHARLES KELLER, JR.
New Orleans, Louisiana

DAVID M. KENNEDY
Salt Lake City, Utah

JAMES R. KENNEDY
Essex Fells, New Jersey

TOM KILLEFER, Chairman Emeritus
United States Trust Company of New York

CHARLES N. KIMBALL, President Emeritus
Midwest Research Institute

HARRY W. KNIGHT, Chairman of the Board
Hillsboro Associates, Inc.

SIGURD S. LARMON
New York, New York

ELMER L. LINDSETH
Cleveland, Ohio

JAMES A. LINEN
Greenwich, Connecticut

GEORGE H. LOVE
Pittsburgh, Pennsylvania

ROY G. LUCKS
San Francisco, California

ROBERT W. LUNDEEN, Retired Chairman
The Dow Chemical Company

FRANKLIN J. LUNDING
Sarasota, Florida

RAY W. MACDONALD, Honorary Chairman of the Board
Burroughs Corporation

IAN MACGREGOR, Former Chairman
AMAX Inc.

MALCOLM MACNAUGHTON, Former Chairman
Castle & Cooke, Inc.

FRANK L. MAGEE
Stahlstown, Pennsylvania

STANLEY MARCUS, Consultant
Carter Hawley Hale Stores, Inc.

AUGUSTINE R. MARUSI, Chairman, Executive Committee
Borden Inc.

OSCAR G. MAYER, Retired Chairman
Oscar Mayer & Co.

L. F. MCCOLLUM
Houston, Texas

JOHN A. MCCONE
Pebble Beach, California

GEORGE C. MCGHEE
Corporate Director and former U.S. Ambassador
Washington, D.C.

CHAMPNEY A. MCNAIR, Vice Chairman
Trust Company of Georgia

J. W. MCSWINEY, Director
The Mead Corporation
Mead World Headquarters

CHAUNCEY J. MEDBERRY III, Chairman, Executive Committee
Bank of America N.T. & S.A.

JOHN. F. MERRIAM
San Francisco, California

LORIMER D. MILTON, Former President
Citizens Trust Company

DON G. MITCHELL
Summit, New Jersey

LEE L. MORGAN, Chairman of the Board, Retired
Caterpillar Tractor Co.

ROBERT R. NATHAN, Chairman
Robert R. Nathan Associates, Inc.

ALFRED C. NEAL
Harrison, New York

J. WILSON NEWMAN, Former Chairman of the Board
Dun & Bradstreet Corporation

THOMAS O. PAINE, President
Thomas Paine Associates

DANIEL PARKER, Honorary Chairman
The Parker Pen Company

JOHN H. PERKINS, Former President
Continental Illinois National Bank and Trust Company of Chicago

HOWARD C. PETERSEN
Radnor, Pennsylvania

C. WREDE PETERSMEYER
Vero Beach, Florida

RUDOLPH A. PETERSON, President (Retired)
Bank of America N.T. & S.A.

DONALD C. PLATTEN, Chairman, Executive Committee
Chemical Bank

R. STEWART RAUCH, Former Chairman
The Philadelphia Saving Fund Society

PHILIP D. REED
New York, New York

AXEL G. ROSIN, Retired Chairman
Book-of-the-Month Club, Inc.

WILLIAM M. ROTH
San Francisco, California

GEORGE RUSSELL
Bloomfield Hills, Michigan

CHARLES J. SCANLON
Essex, Connecticut

JOHN A. SCHNEIDER, President
Warner Amex Satellite Entertainment Company

ELLERY SEDGWICK, JR.
Cleveland Heights, Ohio

ROBERT B. SEMPLE, Retired Chairman
BASF Wyandotte Corporation

LEON SHIMKIN, Chairman Emeritus
Simon and Schuster, Inc.

RICHARD R. SHINN, Former Chairman
Metropolitan Life Insurance Company

WILLIAM P. SIMMONS, Chairman
Trust Company of Middle Georgia

NEIL D. SKINNER
Indianapolis, Indiana

ELLIS D. SLATER
Landrum, South Carolina

DONALD B. SMILEY, Chairman, Finance Committee
R. H. Macy & Co., Inc.

DAVIDSON SOMMERS
Washington, D.C.

ROBERT C. SPRAGUE, Honorary Chairman of the Board
Sprague Electric Company

ELVIS J. STAHR, JR., Partner
Chickering & Gregory

FRANK STANTON, President Emeritus
CBS Inc.

SYDNEY STEIN, JR., Partner
Stein Roe & Farnham

EDGAR B. STERN, JR., President
Royal Street Corporation

J. PAUL STICHT, Chairman, Executive Committee
RJR Nabisco, Inc.

ALEXANDER L. STOTT
Fairfield, Connecticut

C. A. TATUM, JR., Former Chairman
Texas Utilities Company

WAYNE E. THOMPSON, Past Chairman
Merritt Peralta Medical Center

CHARLES C. TILLINGHAST, JR.
Providence, Rhode Island

HOWARD S. TURNER, Retired Chairman
Turner Construction Company

L. S. TURNER, JR.
Dallas, Texas

ROBERT C. WEAVER
New York, New York

JAMES E. WEBB
Washington, D.C.

GEORGE WEISSMAN, Chairman, Executive Committee
Philip Morris Incorporated

WILLIAM H. WENDEL, Vice Chairman
Kennecott Corporation

J. HUBER WETENHALL
New York, New York

GEORGE L. WILCOX, Retired Vice Chairman
Westinghouse Electric Corporation

ARTHUR M. WOOD
Chicago, Illinois

Honorary Trustee on Leave For Government Service

WILLIAM A. HEWITT
U.S. Ambassador to Jamaica

RESEARCH ADVISORY BOARD

Chairman
PAUL W. McCRACKEN
President
American Enterprise Institute
for Public Policy Research

MARTIN FELDSTEIN
President
National Bureau of Economic Research, Inc.

VICTOR R. FUCHS
Professor of Economics
Stanford University

DONALD HAIDER
Professor and Program Director
J. L. Kellogg Graduate School of Management
Northwestern University

PAUL KRUGMAN
Professor of Economics
Sloan School of Management
Massachusetts Institute of Technology

JACK A. MEYER
President
New Directions for Policy

ISABEL V. SAWHILL
Program Director
The Urban Institute

CHARLES L. SCHULTZE
Senior Fellow
The Brookings Institution

PETER O. STEINER
Dean, College of Literature, Science, and the Arts
The University of Michigan

CED PROFESSIONAL AND ADMINISTRATIVE STAFF

ROBERT C. HOLLAND
President

SOL HURWITZ
Senior Vice President and
 Secretary, Board of Trustees

R. SCOTT FOSLER
Vice President and
 Director of Government Studies

ELIZABETH J. LUCIER
Comptroller

KENNETH McLENNAN
Vice President and Director
 of Industrial Studies

CLAUDIA P. FEUREY
Vice President and
 Director of Information

*Advisor on International
Economic Policy*

ISAIAH FRANK
William L. Clayton Professor of
 International Economics
The Johns Hopkins University

NATHANIEL M. SEMPLE
Vice President,
 Secretary, Research and
 Policy Committee, and
 Director of Governmental
 Affairs

PATRICIA O'CONNELL
Vice President and
 Director of Finance

Research
SEONG H. PARK
Economist

LORRAINE M. BROOKER
Economic Research Associate

Research and Policy Committee
PEGGY MORRISSETTE
Deputy Secretary
 and Deputy Director of
 Governmental Affairs

BETTY J. LESLIE
Staff Assistant

Conferences
RUTH MUNSON
Manager

Information and Publications
SANDRA KESSLER HAMBURG
Associate Director

SUZANNE L. DIDIER
Assistant Director

DAVID LUBITZ
Staff Associate

Finance
RUTH KALLA
Deputy Director

DOUGLAS A. STAPLES
Associate Director

AMY JEAN O'NEILL
Campaign Coordinator

Information Services
TIMOTHY J. MUENCH
Manager

Accounting
CATHERINE F. LEAHY
Deputy Comptroller

Administration
THEODORA BOSKOVIC
Administrative Assistant
 to the President

SHIRLEY R. SHERMAN
Administrative Assistant
 to the President

BETTY S. TRIMBLE
Assistant Office Manager

STATEMENTS ON NATIONAL POLICY
ISSUED BY THE RESEARCH AND POLICY COMMITTEE

SELECTED PUBLICATIONS

Leadership for Dynamic State Economies *(1986)*

Tax Reform for a Productive Economy *(1985)*

Investing in Our Children: Business and the Public Schools *(1985)*

Fighting Federal Deficits: The Time for Hard Choices *(1984)*

Strategy for U.S. Industrial Competitiveness *(1984)*

Strengthening the Federal Budget Process:
   A Requirement for Effective Fiscal Control *(1983)*

Productivity Policy: Key to the Nation's Economic Future *(1983)*

Energy Prices and Public Policy *(1982)*

Public-Private Partnership: An Opportunity for Urban Communities *(1982)*

Reforming Retirement Policies *(1981)*

Transnational Corporations and Developing Countries: New Policies for a Changing World Economy *(1981)*

Fighting Inflation and Rebuilding a Sound Economy *(1980)*

Stimulating Technological Progress *(1980)*

Helping Insure Our Energy Future:
   A Program for Developing Synthetic Fuel Plants Now *(1979)*

Redefining Government's Role in the Market System *(1979)*

Improving Management of the Public Work Force:
   The Challenge to State and Local Government *(1978)*

Jobs for the Hard-to-Employ:
   New Directions for a Public-Private Partnership *(1978)*

An Approach to Federal Urban Policy *(1977)*

Key Elements of a National Energy Strategy *(1977)*

The Economy in 1977–78: Strategy for an Enduring Expansion *(1976)*

Nuclear Energy and National Security *(1976)*

Fighting Inflation and Promoting Growth *(1976)*

Improving Productivity in State and Local Government *(1976)*

*International Economic Consequences of High-Priced Energy *(1975)*

Broadcasting and Cable Television:
   Policies for Diversity and Change *(1975)*

Achieving Energy Independence *(1974)*

A New U.S. Farm Policy for Changing World Food Needs *(1974)*

Congressional Decision Making for National Security *(1974)*

*Toward a New International Economic System:
   A Joint Japanese-American View *(1974)*

More Effective Programs for a Cleaner Environment *(1974)*

The Management and Financing of Colleges *(1973)*

Strengthening the World Monetary System *(1973)*

Financing the Nation's Housing Needs *(1973)*

Building a National Health-Care System *(1973)*

*A New Trade Policy Toward Communist Countries *(1972)*

High Employment Without Inflation:
   A Positive Program for Economic Stabilization *(1972)*

Reducing Crime and Assuring Justice *(1972)*

Military Manpower and National Security *(1972)*

The United States and the European Community:
   Policies for a Changing World Economy *(1971)*

Improving Federal Program Performance *(1971)*

Social Responsibilities of Business Corporations *(1971)*

Education for the Urban Disadvantaged:
   From Preschool to Employment *(1971)*

Further Weapons Against Inflation *(1970)*

Making Congress More Effective *(1970)*

Training and Jobs for the Urban Poor *(1970)*

Improving the Public Welfare System *(1970)*

Reshaping Government in Metropolitan Areas *(1970)*

Economic Growth in the United States *(1969)*

Assisting Development in Low-Income Countries *(1969)*

*Nontariff Distortions of Trade *(1969)*

Fiscal and Monetary Policies for Steady Economic Growth *(1969)*

Financing a Better Election System *(1968)*

Innovation in Education: New Directions for the American School *(1968)*

Modernizing State Government *(1967)*

*Trade Policy Toward Low-Income Countries *(1967)*

How Low Income Countries Can Advance Their Own Growth *(1966)*

Modernizing Local Government *(1966)*

Budgeting for National Objectives *(1966)*

*Statements issued in association with CED counterpart organizations in foreign countries.

CED COUNTERPART ORGANIZATIONS IN FOREIGN COUNTRIES

Close relations exist between the Committee for Economic Development and independent, nonpolitical research organizations in other countries. Such counterpart groups are composed of business executives and scholars and have objectives similar to those of CED, which they pursue by similarly objective methods. CED cooperates with these organizations on research and study projects of common interest to the various countries concerned. This program has resulted in a number of joint policy statements involving such international matters as energy, East-West trade, assistance to the developing countries, and the reduction of nontariff barriers to trade.

CE	Círculo de Empresarios Serrano Jover 5-2°, Madrid 8, Spain
CEDA	Committee for Economic Development of Australia 139 Macquarie Street, Sydney 2001, New South Wales, Australia
CEPES	Europäische Vereinigung für Wirtschaftliche und Soziale Entwicklung Reuterweg 14, 6000 Frankfurt/Main, West Germany
IDEP	Institut de l'Entreprise 6, rue Clément-Marot, 75008 Paris, France
経済同友会	Keizai Doyukai (Japan Committee for Economic Development) Japan Industrial Club Building 1 Marunouchi, Chiyoda-ku, Tokyo, Japan
PSI	Policy Studies Institute 100, Park Village East, London NW1 3SR, England
SNS	Studieförbundet Näringsliv och Samhälle Sköldungagatan 2, 11427 Stockholm, Sweden

weeks.
renewed